STO

ACPL ITEM
DISCARDED

IC

AN INTRODUCTORY EXPOSITION OF

Infinite Capitalism

or

The Great Nipple Plot

IC

AN INTRODUCTORY EXPOSITION OF

Infinite Capitalism

OR

The Great Nipple Plot

RICHARD ALTSCHULER

NICHOLAS REGUSH

Little, Brown and Company

Boston • Toronto

Published simultaneously in Canada
by Little, Brown & Company (Canada) Limited

PRINTED IN THE UNITED STATES OF AMERICA

1659372

this book is dedicated to the one i love
JANE   JUNE

Preface

Read this first—do not skip!

For the past eight years we have been developing a perspective of our economy which we feel has revolutionary implications for our conception of ourselves, our morality, and our resulting major institutions — such as the family, religion, and business. After much thought and consultation we at last feel free to reveal the results, being certain that our initial speculations are now firmly on the way to becoming the *facts* of our emerging social structure — which we have designated as *Infinite Capitalism* (IC). As the reader will see for himself in the pages which follow, the implications of this perspective are devastating and total. If the economy continues on its present course, the type of consumer needed to maintain and advance the system will be to Pavlov's conditioned dogs what LSD is to marijuana — for the system of Infinite Capitalism can only maximally develop if Consumer Resistance is eliminated, a process now under way despite sporadic rumblings from such "consumer champions" (*sic*) as Ralph Nader.

Because of the revolutionary implications of our work, all research-and-theory development proceeded in utmost secrecy, and the entire eight-year project was known to those involved by the code name GNP — (the) Great Nipple Plot. To all those who participated in GNP we extend heartfelt congratulations for a secret well kept and a job well done. And now for a few brief words about the book itself.

First, it is essential that this book be read *in the order presented.* A complete understanding of the examples of IC, contained in the second half of the book, cannot be gained if the beginning chapters are skipped over or referred to last. These initial chapters provide the framework and background for what follows. Without a thorough grounding in the theoretical structure of IC, the casual reader is likely to mistake the revolutionary nature of this book for cynicism or even facetiousness.

The first chapter, "ICology," explains the nature of the new science and art of Infinite Capitalism and related aspects, and describes the use of the ICograph, the most complete sales aid yet devised! The next chapter, "TOM" (the) Theory of Morality, explains the nature of the morality which will accompany the full development of IC. The final chapter, "MCA," Market-Creation Analysis, explains the nature of sales techniques consistent with the demands of IC. After reading these chapters, the reader will have a firm understanding and appreciation of his society as it is developing and will gain full benefit and enjoyment from the products and services offered here as examples of the boundless wonders of IC.

R.A. and N.R.

ICological Institute
The Bog
September 1971

CONTENTS

PART ONE

IC in Thought

CHAPTER ONE

ICology

The Two ICologies

ICology is both art and Science, and corresponding to this division are Applied ICology (art) and Theoretical ICology (science). In both instances, ICology considers the interrelationship between several factors (*see* below) in systematic fashion, with the aim of better understanding the economic system in which we live, better predicting future trends, and maximally creating new goods and services for consumption.

ICological Factors

ICology considers the interrelationship between five sets of factors:

(1) infinite technological capacity to produce (IC),

(2) infinite uncertainty/susceptibility among consumers as to what they want or need,

(3) infinite methods of sales promotion (MCA),

(4) infinite morality (IM),

(5) infinite imagination of the entrepreneur.

Noting how these five factors operate in systematic fashion, and then analyzing these factors in light of economic theory for the "system as a whole" are the tasks of Theoretical ICology (TIC). (This present work has not been dedicated to such an exegesis, as this has been reserved for a book now in process, *Theoretical ICology: A Systems Approach to IC.*) But we know, science and art can only be fully separated conceptually, and each is found in the other in *reality*. Thus, the art of ICology (AIC) and the science of ICology (SIC) interpenetrate one another.

The Art of ICology

This particular work has been dedicated to the *art* of infinite capitalism. It is dedicated to *creation*. As such, this work is an attempt to *inspire* the entrepreneur (or entrepreneur-to-be) to utilize his *infinite imagination*. To do this we have heavily utilized *illustration*.

Because we are dealing with a new art form, we have not said everything, we could not say everything, and we did not wish to say everything: we have intentionally been *suggestive*, leaving the mind of the entrepreneur open to the limitless possibilities of IC. Only thus is creativity born.

Applied ICology alerts the entrepreneur to the fact that the system in which he lives has the technological capacity to create infinitely, that consumers in this society don't know what they want or need, and that the morality of this system will self-adjust (*see* "TOM") in accordance with the needs of IC. The entrepreneur is to be *active* in imagining, creating, whatever he loves, wants, or can make profit from; and he must be a *skilled activist* in the art of Market-Creation Analysis (MCA) to guarantee that he will *sell whatever* it is that he produces — whether there is a natural base for it or not!

The ICological Susceptibility Continuum

The artist in ICology (the ICologist) must be extremely sensitive to the nature of consumer uncertainty/susceptibility in contemporary society, for a deep understanding will enable the ICologist to sell anything!

The "infinitely uncertain consumer," not knowing (much of the time) what he wants or needs to satisfy him, is, correspondingly, *infinitely susceptible* to being convinced that he needs whatever it is the producer wishes to sell! The science and art of ICology delineate three major susceptibility levels, ranging from "most susceptible" ("I") to "least susceptible" ("III"). The levels tell the ICologist *the degree to which* designated groups of people will be amenable to, or will resist, being sold a given product or service. These levels complement *the degree of uncertainty* among consumers as to what they want or need.

1. Level III

In this level are the groups *most difficult* (only impossible in the rarest cases) to sell a given product or service. This is because (a) *they cannot use the product or service in question* (e.g., limbless war veterans have no use for the "Anonymous Identity Bracelet," p. 83; (b) *they do not relate to the "general area" of which the product or service is a part* (e.g., "False Nipples" — part of the "sex/fashion area" — will be most difficult to sell to people who are supposedly oblivious to sex and/or who *always wear uniforms*, such as *nuns*); (c) *they relate to the "general area," but they are certain they already know what they need* (e.g., orthodox religionists relate to the "general area" of *"religion"* and are certain they know exactly how to satisfy their religious needs — thus, it will be most difficult to induce these people to use the religious service "Voices Of God," p. 77). For *Susceptibility Level III* people the *strongest* MCA sales techniques will have to be employed (*see* MCA chapter).

2. Level II

In this level are groups who relate to the "general area" of which the product or service is a part, but who have "some ideas of their own" (they are only finitely uncertain) as to what they need within the "general area." Thus, these people are "moderately susceptible" — offering *some* resistance — to the product or service being sold. For example, MCA shows that the "families of corporation executives" do relate to the general area of "gripes against bureaucracies" (*see* "Bureaucracy Gripe Service," p. 35) *but have some ideas of their own* on how to strike back. These people will relate keenly to the idea of the Bureaucracy Gripe Service, but may not immediately buy it. Traditional advertising and moderately strong MCA techniques will convince these people to utilize the Service.

3. Level I

The applied ICologist's dream! In this level are groups who relate to a "general area" but are *infinitely uncertain* as to what they want or need within the "general area." Complementing this infinite uncertainty is *infinite susceptibility!* Level I groups offer virtually no resistance and can be convinced they need anything. For example, MCA shows that (generally) urban females between the ages of 14 and 31 relate very strongly to the "fashion area" but have *"no" definite ideas of their own* as to what they want or need within this area. To return to a previous example, whereas nuns have no need for *False Nipples,* the female now under discussion can be *easily* convinced they *need* false nipples — and this applies *equally* to females with *beautiful* nipples and to females with *unsightly* nipples. Once the question, "What is a beautiful nipple?" has been raised, the infinite process of product creation has begun! (Would anyone argue that there is an *absolute* standard for *the* beautiful nipple?) Level I people have no idea how to answer such a question — leaving the ICologist to answer it for them!

The ICograph

The ICograph is the basic analytical action tool of the IC-Entrepreneur. At a glance the applied ICologist (IC-Entrepreneur) knows at *which groups of people* to direct his sales campaign; *what percentage of the total market* each of these groups represent; and *what MCA techniques* to apply to each of these groups. The ICograph is an *action* aid, and is based upon the results of exceedingly discriminate and in-depth MCA scientific research.

How to Read the ICograph

Following is a blank ICograph. The "vertical side" indicates "percentage of population"; the "horizontal (or bottom) side" indicates both the "Susceptibility Levels" and the "Primary Market Targets"; the "inside" contains the "ICobars." After a few brief comments on the Primary Market Targets and the ICobars, the reader will have mastered the most devastating sales aid yet devised, the ICograph!

ICograph 1

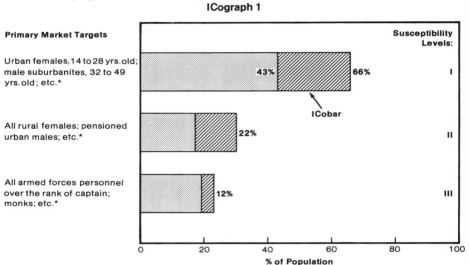

Primary Market Targets

These are the groups of people the applied ICologist will focus upon when selling his product or service. The Primary Market Targets *specify exactly* which groups are "most infinitely susceptible" to being convinced they need a given product or service; "moderately infinitely susceptible"; and "least infinitely susceptible." In many cases the designated target group will immediately "make sense" to the reader:

i.e., the connection, or lack of it, between the target group and the product/service will be *logical*. For example, people who hold *college degrees* are immediately recognizable as a "Susceptibility Level III" group (least infinitely susceptible) when considering the *Degree-Faking Service* (p. 61); on the other hand, there is *no* immediately apparent reason why stockbrokers are "Level I" (infinitely susceptible) when considering the *Personalized Soap-Opera Service*. YET, IN STUDY AFTER STUDY, THIS IS WHAT MCA IN-DEPTH RESEARCH REVEALS. Finally, the groups designated as *Primary Market Targets* are only those whose *numbers were large enough to* be worthwhile listing; if it was found, for example, that a group was "infinitely susceptible" but only had, say, 18 members, we did not feel it to be notable enough to include in the ICograph.

The ICobar

The ICobar tells at a glance: (a) the *exact* % of the *total* U.S. buying population for each Susceptibility Level; (b) the *exact* % that the *Primary Market Targets* (for each Susceptibility Level) contribute to this total. Looking at the ICobar, the reader will notice that it is divided into *two* distinct areas; from the *base* of the ICograph to the end of the first area (where the "clear" or "blank" space ends) is the % of the population contributed by the Primary Market Targets; the remaining area ("shaded") represents that % of the total population which we have not designated under the market targets either because the people were *randomly distributed throughout the population* or because there was a *multitude of groups,* none of which was large enough to be worthwhile listing.

A Practice Reading

Looking under Susceptibility Level I (blank ICograph), the applied ICologist sees immediately that (a) the Primary Market Targets encompass 43% of the total population of the U.S. (about 90 million people); (b) the total % of people who are "infinitely susceptible" (Level I) is 66% of the U.S. population (about 120 million people). The applied ICologist therefore knows that 66% of the U.S. population is found to be "infinitely susceptible" to being convinced they need the product or service in question, and *he knows exactly who 43% of this 66% is.* The ICologist will thus know to focus his sales campaign on the 43%, and depend upon "spill-over," etc., to reach the remaining 23% (the difference between 43% and 66%). The same interpretation is applied to all Susceptibility Levels for all the products and services.

The careful reader will soon master the ICograph's use and should have a "feel" for what went into it and what it fully represents. The ICograph is the indispensable aid of the action-oriented ICologist saving his time and money, and guaranteeing sales success. The ICograph says "GO!!!!" The time to begin is now!

A Strange Feeling

The ICologist must be aware that any goods or services can potentially be directed at groups in all three susceptibility levels. Once this susceptibility continuum is understood, and once the powers of our technology are comprehended, a strange feeling overcomes one, as the realization dawns that one is leaving an "old reality" — finite capitalism — and has entered a "new reality" — *infinite* capitalism. Those who come to possess the *ICological* reality soon realize there is no need to "hold back."

IC Illustrated

The IC-Principle has been illustrated in the body of this work in order to say what "cannot be said." Age-old wisdom assures us that *illustrations* are more effective in creating a reality than analyses such as the one presented in this chapter.

To understand IC fully, one must not only understand it "with the mind," one must also have an "intuitive" understanding: this is the nature of *Art!*

A Note on Further Reading

Two questions that the reader may wish answered at this point are (1) if one is dealing (especially) with a "Susceptibility Level III" group, how does the ICologist actually induce these people to buy (that is, how does he *create* the market)? The answer to this is given in the "MCA" chapter (Chapter 3). How does one who feels compelled to *justify* certain *innovative*, but necessary, MCA activities and certain products and/or services do so in light of existing morality? The answers to these questions are found in the "TOM" Chapter (Chapter 2).

CHAPTER TWO

TOM: (The) Theory of Morality

*Any System of Behavior Contains the Seeds
of Its Own Morality. This Is TOM.*

IC and IM

Any system of behavior, be it feudalism, tribalism, Communism, Nazism, democracy, etc., contains the seeds of its own morality. Finite Capitalism contained the seeds of its own morality, though we never saw a complete flowering of these seeds.

IC contains the seeds of its own morality; as a system of behavior, IC contains the moral justification for its existence and growth. This moral justification and statement of ideals is *IM: Infinite Morality.* In simple terms (a more technical explanation will be afforded in the forthcoming *Intellectual's TOM*) this means that a system of behavior based upon a principle of infinity (IC) calls forth a system of morals based upon the same meta-foundation, or IM. Anything short of this would contradict the *inherent logic* of the system, and be at variance with the universal law of morality as succinctly stated by TOM.

The "Morality Gap"

We are now witnessing the incipient stages of both IC and IM: both can be seen emerging "simultaneously" by astute observers, with IM somewhat behind IC developmentally.

There is always a *time lag* between any set of behaviors and the morality appropriate to it, simply because behaviors change faster than ideas, values, attitudes, etc. This phenomenon may be termed the *Morality Gap*. Depending upon circumstances, this gap is always greater or smaller. For finite capitalism it was always rather large.

As any set of behaviors is in constant flux, the moral structure is likewise in constant flux, but at a slower rate. Sometimes behavioral systems change so rapidly, owing to factors such as technological advances, material catastrophes, and the like, that the moral system at any given time appears to be completely inappropriate for the times. When this occurs, there will be general confusion among the people because they will be doing certain things but believing others.

No matter how great the morality gap, however, there is a tendency inherent in any behavior system for the morality system to tend toward *maximum consistency*.

Doubting TOMists

The historical and sociological evidence for TOM is so great that it can only be denied on emotional — sometimes called spiritual — grounds. There are always those who doubt the existence of even the most clear-cut phenomena simply because it is their nature to doubt. These individuals will, like all programmed machines, do what they *must*, and to these *doubting TOMists* we extend the invitation to challenge the theory here being presented.

The Present System

In our present system we are witnessing a moral gap which is now in the process of self-correction. This is a state in which the morality appropriate to finite capitalism, a morality based upon *finite* principles (not *all* behaviors are viewed as virtuous) and on remnants of the also-dated Judeo-Christian moral structure, is at variance with the emerging system of infinite behaviors in the economic sphere — which, of course, has primary influence on all other institutions in society. The effect of this variance is that the finite moral structure (now in the process of flux) is having its "draw-back" effects, in that it is slightly impeding the development of infinite productive capacity which is now firmly, if not fully, entrenched. This effect of the moral system on the behavioral system is a commonplace and expected phenomenon, limited as the phenomenon always proves itself to be.

A Primitive Way of Thinking: Guilt

A major reason for the present "gap" is that some capitalist entrepreneurs feel *guilt* (the old, finite moral structure) when engaging in certain business ventures based upon the infinity principle (*see*, for example, in this work, The Death Simulation Service). Thus, the finite, guilt-ridden moral structure is a draw-back. Clearly, the technological capacity to create any good or service, and the need for that good or service, an infinite process of capitalist growth potential, cannot (and will not) be held back by an archaic (when viewed in the 1970's) value system; if the economic system — both with respect to production and need creation (MCA) — lauds any series of behaviors as appropriate, then the moral structure must also, by law, conform to it!

IM and the Law

Certain of the products and/or services which will be created under the IC-Principle *could possibly* be interpreted by some as illegal; and some of the methods appropriate to MCA — e.g., drug therapy — *could possibly* be interpreted as illegal. The development of IM, however, will negate this possibility.

It is vital to understand that a behavior itself is never what is immoral and/or illegal; rather, it is the way in which a given behavior is defined by others, particularly those aligned with the law. At the most obvious level, if a soldier kills someone his action is usually defined as heroic and patriotic, but if a ghetto dweller kills someone it is murder; if a "citizen" forcibly takes money from someone it is robbery, but if the government does the same thing it is "taxation." The number of *interpretations possible* about a given behavior is endless, and thus the "morality" or "legality" of a given behavior depends upon (1) who is doing the interpreting, and (2) the standards for morality-legality.

What is being said, then, is that nothing in MCA or IC is *in itself* immoral and/or illegal! Not, at least, until someone defines the behaviors that way. The development of IM will ensure favorable definitions to those engaging in behaviors supportive of the "System" of Infinite Capitalism. This process of favorable definitions applied to behaviors which are questionable can be seen in our present (finite) system of Big Business, Big Labor, and Big Government — three large organizations which have turned morality upside down, and which have paved the way for the development of a truly endless series of moral interpretations.

Thus, within the system of infinite morality such MCA methods as threat of harm, mental anguish, brainwashing, even actual physical harm, are all respectable activities — or on their way to becoming them. The ICologist will thus study these processes, enabling him to encourage *faster development* of infinite morality, which is now emerging under its own momentum.

This Is TOM!

In sum, TOM makes it clear that we will witness the development of a full-blown morality appropriate to the infinite system of economic behaviors of which the United States is capable — and which it needs.

This system of morality will tell us, plainly and simply, that whatever is done is good. It will also tell us that whatever *can* be done is good!

When a system depends upon infinite productive economic relations and is based upon a moral structure which is finite, the system operates at less than full momentum, and those who man the system are guilt-ridden and confused, and ultimately become hostile (as a result of their own frustrations). In our times, this contradiction will self-correct through the development of an infinite morality.

ANY SYSTEM OF BEHAVIOR CONTAINS THE SEEDS OF ITS OWN MORALITY. *This* is TOM!

CHAPTER THREE

MCA: Market-Creation Analysis

A Series of Infinite *Research Methods and Selling Techniques Used by Entrepreneurs or ICological Specialists to Induce People to Purchase a Product or Utilize a Service: This Is MCA.*

How Does MCA Differ from MR (Market Research)?

Market Research attempts to discover through the use of traditional social scientific methods *which* individuals are "ready" to buy *what* — and nothing more. "*What do people prefer?*" e.g., green or red lettering on the "Faz" box. "*What are people ready to buy?*" "*What are people uncertain about?*" "*What fears and insecurities do people have that can be played upon?*" (Cigarettes sell popularity, cosmetics sell beauty, etc.) These are the common questions raised by the market researcher. For example, it was once discovered that certain types of insecure women stopped buying Jell-O because Jell-O commercials made Jell-O *too beautiful.*

Through the careful use of depth research, market researchers gather data on secret distresses, self-images, human impulses, the act of upward striving, hidden aversions, and hedonistic factors, and modern advertising uses this information to *woo* the consumer who is *more* or *less* ready to buy something.

MCA Explained

The key word in the definition of MCA, of course, is *"infinite."* Whereas, *Market Research* and *Advertising* are *limited* to *orthodox research* and *action* practices based on present-day moral standards, laws, guilt, habit, ignorance, and outdated economic thinking (all these are Post-Industrial Capitalism [PIC] *inhibitions*), MCA uses *all* traditional MR (Market Research) techniques *but goes infinitely beyond the Great Hold-Back Factor* (GHF).

The Great Hold-Back Factor Revealed:
GHF = MR — IC-consciousness — TOM.

EXAMINING THE FACTOR. Market Creation Analysis (MCA) not only focuses on who is more or less *ready* (like MR) to buy a product but focuses on who can be *made* to buy a product or use a service *by any means necessary.* MCA not only "woos" an already existing market but also *creates its own market.* It is precisely *this act of creation* that allows the analyst to cross the holdback barrier of traditionality and limitation. MCA *forces* (if necessary) a target group of consumers to believe that they need, or even anxiously demand, a product or service — *whatever it may be!* It is not that the techniques (*see* below) that characterize the action phase of

MCA are *totally* new to sales, for the present *finite* system of capitalism and MR use all the techniques in adumbrated or modified form; the difference is that MCA *sheds the veil of hypocrisy* and unabashedly uses these techniques *to their fullest potential.*

THE ACTION PHASE (operating beyond the GHF). MCA particularly works on those people it designates as the "infinitely susceptible"—people who have no idea what they need or want. Although for any given product and at any given time such people may be members of a particular age group, sex, social class, race, religion, etc., the *infinitely susceptible* may also include the "barely educable," the mentally feeble, the psychotically insecure, the diseased, and so on. Such people *will* be convinced they need anything you wish to sell. (It should be noted that while the above groups are not intrinsically necessary for the success of IC, their numbers *have* expanded rapidly during this transitional era and they *are* usually "infinitely susceptible.")

The "levels of susceptibility" are discovered through specific questionnaires administered in the most profitable social scientific manner. As noted above, some individuals may be judged as infinitely susceptible, others as moderately infinitely susceptible, and still others as *"not" susceptible at all* (least infinitely susceptible). These degrees of susceptibility, commonly viewed by ICologists as the complement of the *Consumer Uncertainty Factor,* are deduced by using both objective and subjective research criteria. While the discreet and sophisticated statistical analyses used by an ICological expert in the course of MCA cannot be usefully replicated here, perhaps a simplified example will demonstrate the basic procedure. If a respondent answers "almost never" when questioned whether she is "ever lonely," the MCA analyst seeks "objective" criteria such as whether or not she keeps old photographs, reads Rod McKuen poetry, *Cosmopolitan*, etc., and thus arrives at a balanced final judgment as to the individual's susceptibility to the "Loneliness Service."*

With carefully researched data, MCA *can cross the Factor Line* and swing into action. The following are well-conceived MCA action categories: the *Shameless Factor, Physical Harm, Threat, Outright Lying,* and *Concentration-Camp Methods.* The motto for the action phase is *"All the Way with MCA."*

At first sight the action techniques presented below may seem immoral and/or illegal — *look again!* These techniques are merely extensions of what precisely exists in modified form, though in many instances they are employed freely. For example, religious organizations — among the most enduring and successful enterprises known to modern man — freely employ *shameless factors* and *threat of physical harm* to sell their products and services; many large corporations and all branches of government have employed all action techniques freely, especially *outright lying, brainwashing,* and *physical harm* — and they have been doing this for decades; cigarette companies have been appealing to *youngsters* to form a *habit* — a clear instance of *"drug therapy."* In addi-

---

* To date, all MCA research has been conducted at the ICological Institute, The Bog; following the publication of this and abovementioned subsequent volumes, training *and franchises* for MCA Centers will be offered to selected progressive social scientists. These Centers will then serve as consultants to would-be IC-Entrepreneurs, providing complete ICographic studies — including specially tailored ICographs — for whatever product/service the IC-Entrepreneur desires.

tion to these *actual* practices, the *dynamics of history* (TOM) make it clear that these techniques will soon evolve full-scale on their own.

If you have reservations about employing any of these techniques, the best advice is to *start slowly*, e.g., tell *small* lies; you will soon realize others are, and have been, doing this successfully for years. Then, "step up" the lies a level or two. In no time at all you will be "infinitely lying" — in conformance with the IC-Principle. The same advice applies to all the other action techniques. After a short while you will realize you are part of a "historical current," and you — and everyone else — will come to see these activities as both moral and legal and necessary for the perpetuation of the emerging system of Infinite Capitalism.

The Shameless Factor

In accordance with the Infinity Principle, *shame* is taken to its logical conclusion as the consumer is made to feel *totally* useless, inadequate, ugly, and so on. With proper media utilization, this approach will be devastating. At the time of this writing, the *midi* has been successfully resisted by consumers. This was largely due to the *Great Hold-Back Factor*. If women are to be convinced to buy, *no one* in a *target* sample should be spared *extreme insult; Creative Abuse* is the Shameless Factor Key.

Outright Lying

Basically an old technique, it includes false claims of product durability, usefulness, results, beauty, false endorsements by physicians and other "experts," and false promises of bonuses for buying the product or service.

Threat

Threat can be applied to virtually anyone about anything, is easy to apply, is recommended to be used freely, in particular with those who are suspicious and highly susceptible to threats. Such people not only include the traditionally religious but also believers in such things as astrology, the industrial-military complex, and the Mafia. Threats of disease, chastisement, permanent suffering, bad luck, or death will be implied if purchase is not made. MCA can also employ incremental harassment — as, for instance, through the mails. (The mass magazines have already developed the technique — through computers — of huge mailings, each letter addressed personally and containing a message that mentions the recipient's neighbors or associates.

Physical Harm

In order to maintain the integrity of the Threat Factor, it will undoubtedly on occasion be necessary to use Physical Harm. Although there might be a rare instance when it will be directed against an individual, for the most part — in the American tradition — while initiated by business groups, it will be carried out by government agencies and directed at identifiable groups, e.g., students, workers, housewives.

Concentration Camp Methods

These methods include drug "therapy" hypnosis, Pavlovian conditioning, and brainwashing. Here again, the unsophisticated observer is likely to believe that these methods are cruel, bizarre, and unlikely to be used. But the student of ICology not only sees them as the epitome of the ICological method; he appreciates their long and honorable history. First came the repetitive and "seemingly inane" jingles, rhymes, and songs that sold tons of soap, toothpaste, and patent medicines, not by providing information but simply by going round in otherwise empty heads. Then there was the noble but abortive attempt at subliminal television advertising. The cosmetic, followed closely by the fashion, industry provided numerous early examples of attempts at mass conditioning. Of course, it has been the tobacco industry, as noted above, that has led the way in drug therapy. Its successes have been so outstanding that it requires special mention.

Among the less sophisticated economic and consumer analysts exists the belief, albeit mistaken, that the gigantic success of tobacco is caused solely, or predominately, by its addictive characteristics. While we would not wish to underestimate the obvious asset of addictiveness, one should not overlook tobacco's weaknesses. First, until the user becomes addicted — that is, until he has used the product for a considerable period of time — he has *no need or use* for it at all. Second, the initial use of the product is invariably accompanied by coughing fits, nausea, and dizziness. Third, it has been established that prolonged use contributes to lung cancer, emphysema, and heart disease. Any industry that can create a market of millions for such a product deserves due credit.

The techniques used to create this market are appropriate and informative. Only an instinctive awareness of ICology could have led tobacco executives to associate their product simultaneously with both masculinity and femininity, sociability and introspectiveness. Without realizing the importance of the step, the industry has made a tentative trip across the *Great Hold-Back Factor* (GHF): adopting the distribution techniques of its competition (illegal drugs), it has offered *free samples*. It is only fitting to note here that any society that permits an entrepreneur openly to offer gift packages of a deadly, addictive drug provides outstanding proof of TOM and the accelerating transition to IC.

A Note on the Above Skills

MCA analysts need to develop carefully skills for utilizing these action techniques and for developing others. Creative application of these techniques, such as juxtaposing brainwashing and physical harm, for example, or possibly all five action techniques, is the key to becoming a successful ICologist. The possible combinations and permutations follow the IC-Principle, allowing for infinite development by the artistic and industrious entrepreneur.

A Final Note on the Use of This Book

Each of the following products and services is described in the form of a data sheet such as a salesman for the product or service might carry. The first section contains a definition of the product or service, a summary of the Market Creation techniques, and the essential, corresponding ICograph. This material is then followed by an "Exposition" section, which delves into the MCA thought and philosophy behind the product/service. While the "Exposition" is not essential to successful marketing of the product or service, it provides examples of the new modes of thought essential to the neophyte ICologist.

PART TWO

IC in Action

CHAPTER FOUR

False Nipples

Product

False Nipples

Function and Nature

An enhancing cosmetic and/or clothing accessory: to increase sexual attractiveness; to provide psychological aid to females with inhibitions who want to be fashionable; to alleviate physical discomfort; general novelty.

Market Creation

The nipple is the focal point in fashion's newest style: the nude, or bra-less, look. Fashion has always dictated one or another part of the body — mouth, bosom, legs, etc. — as the central locus of "chicness" and/or sexuality. Once that locus has been established, the public clamors for devices, methods, or treatments to enhance their personal loci. Today, all eyes are fixed on the nipple, a part of the body for which no objective standards of beauty exist. False Nipples, the enhancers, direct themselves at (1) women's fear of having unsightly and/or small nipples; (2) psychological inhibitions; (3) sensitive nipples. MCA conclusively shows that artificial products which enhance beauty and sexual attractiveness — falsies, false hair, false derrières, etc. — have been highly successful in American society. Since the primary need for false nipples has been created by a change in the fashion industry, distribution and promotion of the false nipples could proceed most efficiently via the fashion industry. No similar products exist which serve the same function as the false nipples.

ICograph 2

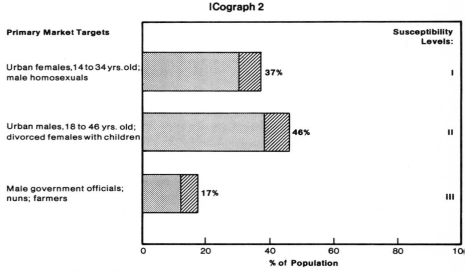

Exposition

Background: The Bra-less Look in Fashions

Several years ago a movement started among young females, roughly 14 to 28 years of age, to abandon the brassiere — an item which many females saw as physically constraining, psychologically constraining, or both. About the same time that this "female liberation movement" was gaining momentum, the fashion industry introduced the "nude look" — and the most popular apparel became the *see-through blouse*. This, too, encouraged many females to abandon the brassiere. The bra-less look is now more popular than ever, and unless finite marketing techniques disrupt the process, all evidence indicates that this trend will continue.

Why? What is the appeal of the bra-less look? Most obviously, it allows for *increased sexual appeal*, for more widespread leverage in the "sexual marketplace." No-bra, especially in conjunction with the see-through blouse, allows the female to bring the "negligée look" into the streets. Second, as already mentioned, the bra-less look affords a certain degree of freedom.

Older females, those between the ages of 29 and 34, have also been adopting the bra-less look. Foremost among the reasons is that many of these women are getting divorced (or fear divorce), have children, and find the need to attract males (ultimately with marriage in mind) most urgent. With the ratio of females to males increasing, divorced females with children, as well as childless females in this age group, find any device a valuable one which can be used to attract eligible males. The bare-breasted look, with nipples exposed, is currently a favorite. But this raises the question, "What is a beautiful nipple?" There is, of course, no certain answer as to what a really beautiful, sexy nipple looks like — and such doubt, when exposed, is a sure harbinger of IC.

The False Nipple as a Solution to Problems

The bra-less look has resulted in several "natural problem areas" — and this look easily allows for the *creation* of other problems. All of these problems, in turn, result in the demand for *solutions:* and the solutions lie, of course, with *false nipples.*

THREE TYPES OF PROBLEMS. Generally speaking, most problems may be subsumed under three headings: physical discomfort, physical appearance, psychological discomfort.

1. *Physical Discomfort.* As a result of not wearing a brassiere, many females report pain, discomfort, or chafing resulting from the *exposed nipples* rubbing against the blouse material. This problem, not anticipated in advance, has become a major one.

2. *Physical Appearance.* There are many females who want to wear the see-through blouse and no brassiere, but who are not sure their nipples are as *attractive* as they could be. This problem has two aspects: on the one hand, there is the female who would prefer that her nipples be more *shapely,* a different *color* or *tone,* a different *texture,* etc.; on the other hand, there is the female who is dissatisfied with the *size* of her nipples, feeling, most often, that they are too small. Many females who have tiny nipples, no larger than the average male's nipples, feel that males do not find such nipples stimulating. However, opinions vary, as many males *do* find such nipples stimulating. This point is emphasized here, because a good part of the prospective market for false nipples includes such females with tiny nipples, and the way in which such nipples are perceived and evaluated by both males and females will play a major part in determining sales.

3. *Psychological Discomfort.* There are many females with psychological resistance to exposing their nipples, even fe-

males who may have beautiful nipples. In spite of this, some females expose themselves, but suffer for it; others, who would like to expose themselves but can't, also suffer psychologically. Our market-creation analysis indicates that many females who feel psychologically ill at ease about their *real* nipples would feel *no inhibition about exposing a false nipple!* Many females feel no inhibition about exposing something *they* know is not their own — but they don't mind if others think it's "the real thing." This is a rather common psychological process. For example, many females will not wear a bizarre hairdo if it is designed from their own hair, but feel no reservations about wearing such a hairdo if it is a wig!

False nipples, which would be made to look and feel (through blouse materials) like the real nipples, and which would simply "paste over" the real nipples, or be inserted into "pockets" in blouses, sweaters, etc., is quite obviously the natural solution to the three problem areas identified. At the present moment there is *no product* on the market which directs itself to these problems.

False-Nipple Growth

Although the number of females who now actually wear the nude look, or who do not wear a brassiere, is relatively small, this number is growing rapidly. The real leap in growth, however, will take place *once the false nipple is introduced to the buying public!* Once introduced, appropriate MCA techniques will encourage females who to this point would love to wear nude fashions or abandon the bra, but who have not done so (because of unsightly nipples, sensitive nipples, or inhibitions), to do so! Such females will find, with their embarrassment or pain gone — made obsolete by the false nipple — that there is no reason *not* to expose the breasts.

A Note on Nipple-Variation Possibilities

The extent of product variation possible with the false nipples conforms to the principle of IC — and thus allows for (theoretically) Infinite Growth Potential (IGP). Unlike the real nipples, the false nipples could easily vary in the following attributes: size, color, texture, and shape. Thus, the false nipple market could diversify endlessly, depending upon what is "in" at a given moment, or WHAT THE PRODUCER CREATES AS "IN." As the history of product variation in this country has shown, the smallest differences can be employed as major selling points. Consequently, a false nipple with *freckles* could possibly become a sales "rage." Likewise, one could easily create varying *Lines*, as is done in fashions and cosmetics: color coordination, costume variation, etc. One type of nipple could be appropriate for sheer blouses, another for ribbed sweaters, another for denim workshirts.

So far as color coordination goes, the possibilities are endless: with a light-blue sheer blouse, for example, a dark blue or aqua nipple would look beautiful; likewise, the female who dyes her hair red might want nipples to match or complement the hair change; another possibility is the Black Is Beautiful nipple, etc. Market-Creation-Analysis (MCA) could easily create an endless demand in this area.

Taking off on another Line, the "built-in nipple" would revolutionize the fashion industry. If a designer, for example, felt that his dress would look best with a "low-nipple look," it would be designed with the nipple already "built in" to the dress.

Market Permanency

Generally speaking, the bulk of the false-nipple market will be "permanent" so long as the bra-less look remains permanent and/or nude fashions remain permanent.* But, as we have indicated, these fashion looks are most definitely on the upsurge, not only in our own society, but *in other societies as well.* This means, of course, that the false nipple has tremendous *export-possibilities* in societies with as much fashion freedom as our own.

Geographic Factors

Although we envisage the false nipple as a "steady" market item, it should be mentioned that sales will fluctuate owing to geographic factors in certain sectors of the country, particularly those sectors with wide changes in seasons. During cold weather, of course, the nude look is rarely worn (an opportunity for some daring MCA!) and consequently there would be little need for false nipples in this respect. However, many females still wear no brassiere in cold weather, and the nipples would look especially effective under say, a sweater (it is possible that a special nipple could be created for winter clothing). Other sectors of the country will allow for see-through fashions all year round, and it is here where sales will be the greatest.

---

* Although MCA could keep the false nipple a market success without the bra-less look, large initial expenditures would be necessary with the "natural base" gone.

Distribution

As has been mentioned, the false nipple is a "derivative product" in that the need for the nipple has been created by changes in the fashion industry. Consequently, distribution of false nipples could proceed most easily through clothing manufacturers producing nude fashions (including brassiere manufacturers making see-through bras) and the cosmetic industry, which follows fashion and has wider distribution.

CHAPTER FIVE

Bureaucracy Gripe Service

Service

Bureaucracy Gripe Service

Function and Nature

An antibureaucratic tactical information and consulting service to provide citizens who have gripes against bureaucracies with the know-how to *strike back*.

Market Creation

A study of the relationship between Man and Bureaucracy shows that Man is highly alienated from large bureaucracies, has many major gripes against them, and desires to strike back but does not know how. The Bureaucracy Gripe Service — using the inherent weaknesses of the bureaucracy — provides such knowledge, centering its attention on three major aspects of bureaucracies: computers, staff, and environment. Strike-backs range from mild "get-evens" to "shutting it down." The Service will be staffed with ex-bureaucrats who either left their jobs voluntarily or were "dismissed." Such people provide firsthand knowledge and inside information on how to strike back effectively. There is a phenomenal business opportunity for the ICologist to export this Service to the "emerging nations" just beginning to bureaucratize, and to get in on the *ground floor* in defining and creating gripes — and what to do about them!

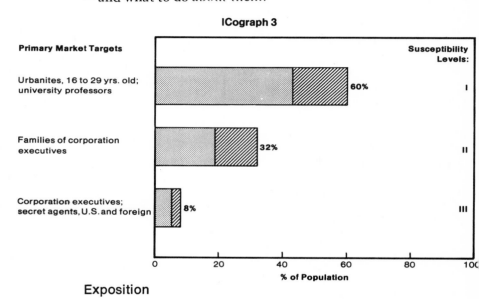

ICograph 3

Primary Market Targets

Susceptibility Levels:

Urbanites, 16 to 29 yrs. old; university professors — 60% — I

Families of corporation executives — 32% — II

Corporation executives; secret agents, U.S. and foreign — 8% — III

% of Population

Exposition

Facts About Gripes

A subject which has preoccupied social scientists is the relationship betwen Man and Bureaucracy: the conclusions generally reached are that Man is highly alienated from bureaucracies, resents them, but is powerless in the face of them. MCA inquired to find out exactly how deeply these gripes were held by the general public, and concluded: (1) 79.3 to

92.2% of all adults have "major" gripes against one or more bureaucracies; (2) 2 out of every 26.7 people desire "strongly" to *strike back*; (3) *how* to strike back is highly problematic for all people (save 3.2% in the "beyond griping" category who have decided to use violent means).

The obvious conclusion to be drawn from the above is that many Americans are either ready now for or *can be made to desire* a service which would provide them with the know-how to strike back. The "Bureaucracy Gripe Service" is suggested here as an IC-Natural, requiring minimal capital to initiate and develop successfully.

Staffing the Gripe Service

The Gripe Service will be staffed most easily and effectively from among the ranks of the "bureaucratic dispossessed." These are individuals — men and women, young and old, executives and rank and file, technicians and administrators — who either were "dismissed" or voluntarily left bureaucracies and who now despise them. MCA has found that among the roughly 700,000 people who were either fired from or quit bureaucracies in the past 2 years, 95.1% would "love to strike back effectively" (both as former employees and as citizens-at-large). These individuals, who occupied different positions in the hierarchy, can provide the necessary firsthand information to clients wishing to strike back effectively.

The Range of Strike-Back Opportunities

There are many ways to strike back against bureaucracies, and the particular strategy decided upon should be consistent with the nature of the gripe as presented by the client. The range goes from mild "get-evens" to "cessation of operations." All of the means suggested are "nonviolent," though *unintended consequences* (more commonly known as *serendipitous happenstances*) cannot, by definition, be predicted in advance.

The mildest form of "get-even" would simply be registering the gripe with the *appropriate* person. Thus, if it is a vice president that the client wishes to "gripe out," the B.G.S. would provide the client with the *name* of the V.P. and either the *direct phone number* in his/her office, or a number at *home*. This will counter the all-too-frustrating experience of having to "gripe out" a secretary or switchboard operator, neither of whom is your desired target. Most often one has to get past countless secretaries to reach a V.P. ("the larger the bureaucracy, the more secretaries between the client and the V.P." — otherwise known as *Richnick's Law*), only to be told that "the vice president is 'out' " or " 'cannot be reached at the moment.' " These problems are eliminated with direct dialing or the "at home" approach.

If the B.G.S. is well staffed, and represents a wide range of bureaucracies, it is likely that some staff member will be familiar, based upon previous job experience, with the *particular sensitivities* of the V.P. or president in question. Should this be the case, for an additional fee commensurate with the problem to be solved, the client can be provided with the information to "ripen" the gripe. For example, if it is known that V.P. "X" from a given department store is having difficulties with his wife, the client can be informed of this and ripen the gripe-out by casually mentioning this along with the gripe: e.g., "The way your store is managed, no wonder your wife Mildred complains about you."

If the client's gripe is of a more serious nature and is directed at the "bureaucracy in general," there are many, many ways to "cause trouble" for those working in the bureaucracy and those who possibly benefit from it (some clients perhaps), or "shut it down" (to borrow a phrase from the young radicals of today). The staff of the B.G.S., if it is worth its salt, will know how to use the *inherent* weaknesses of the bureaucracy to bring about its "disruption" and/or "fall."

Three major areas to be focused upon within the bureaucracy are the *computer*, the *staff*, and the *environment*. Most personally satisfying strike-backs will be aimed at the staff-environment eco-unit, since the client can personally *be there* to participate in, and witness, the strike-back. The computer will not be emphasized here, as it is assumed that the general public — through means such as writing wrong amounts on money orders, adding extra holes to computer cards, etc. — is skilled in this area (the Service, however, will be able to suggest "less common" computer-disruption techniques).

The Staff

Most bureaucratic staffs are *conditioned to act* in a particular fashion at a particular time, even when events have changed markedly to require *different* behaviors (this is known as "trained incapacity"). When the bureaucratic staff does *not* change, chaos or malfunctioning generally results. The staff of the B.G.S. can suggest ways that the client or B.G.S. staff member (depending upon the request of the client) can effectively create a *disorienting scenario* with which the conditioned bureaucrat cannot cope. It is suggested that the *client* play out the scenario so that he/she can be there to *watch* the confusion (the scenario could also be played out at the *home* of the bureaucrat. This could possibly require "scenario training," which would be provided — for a fee — by the Service.) For example, the client could begin a "conversation with God" in a loud and emphatic voice, accompanied by frenzied gestures, directly in the middle of a heavily occupied work area of the bureaucracy in question. This would stop work operations and upset everyone. The scenario method is *legal* and achieves the desired results.

The Environment

Most bureaucrats think of themselves as very civilized people, above the lower animals and nonbureaucrats, and the *interior* of most large bureaucracies reinforces this image; the interior environments are *antiseptic*. Because this image is rooted so deeply in the psyche of the bureaucrat, it is rarely discussed consciously — and yet the smooth functioning of the bureaucracy depends upon an antiseptic environment to reinforce this image. The crux of the matter is that the bureaucracy can be viewed as a device to *eliminate emotion* from human relationships, and thus by "injecting emotion" into it, disruption or destruction becomes predictable.

For example, *foul odors*, if unleashed in a bureaucracy, would subtly change the environment so that work operations could not continue. This could be most effectively and legally carried out by having the client enter the bureaucracy neatly dressed *but smelling foully*. Similarly, *noises* will disrupt the bureaucracy, and thus the client could play out a "crying-baby scenario" by simply entering with crying babies (the more the merrier). Other possible and easy-to-carry-out scenarios are having the client "play deaf" and thus make everyone scream — a particularly effective scenario if the client complains of something embarrassing to the bureaucracy, e.g., overcharging; also, the client could enter with a lot of yelping animals. In another vein, the client could vomit in the middle of a work area, while continually complaining of his "medical problem," *ad ic.*

Exporting the Bureaucracy Gripe Service

For those who want to get in on the *ground floor* of things, the B.G.S. can fruitfully be set up in the "emerging nations" which are just *beginning* to bureaucratize. In such countries as India, Paraguay, Ceylon, etc., the rise of bureaucracies will bring untold problems to the people, and the B.G.S. can be there *from the beginning* to bring to consciousness the nature of the gripes encountered, and to let the people know they can strike back. The opportunity to get in on the ground floor was missed in our Western culture; it would be a business disaster to allow it to happen again.

Needless to say, the Service is easily exportable to already bureaucratized societies such as Germany, France, England, etc., which have comparable problems to the U.S.

CHAPTER SIX

Personalized Soap-Opera Service

Service

Personalized Soap-Opera Service

Function and Nature

A computerized creative-writing agency which produces standardized and/or uniquely written soap-opera scripts fashioned after the personal life-events of the client and which functions to satisfy the need of the individual to see himself/herself as the "center" of a dramatic script; to "objectify" the individual's "life drama" so that others may appreciate the individual's "private struggle."

Market Creation

The great appeal of the soap opera is based upon the fact that it adequately and dramatically reflects real-life situations of millions of individuals, and, most important, it makes the individual's suffering and sacrifice seem important. Research reveals that the normal individual "projects" himself into scripts of various kinds, indicating a need to be the "center" of a "life drama," and to see himself "objectively." These factors provide the basis for the Personalized Soap-Opera Service. Such a Service, staffed with skilled soap-opera writers and an A-1361-TX computer, will create a soap-opera script for the client in question in which the client is the "hero" or "heroine." The Service is simple to initiate and guarantees a handsome profit potential.

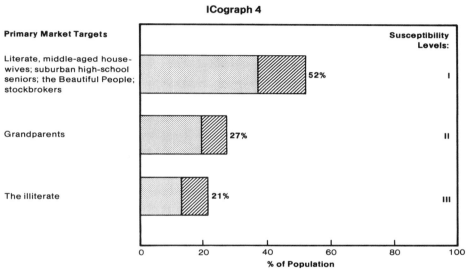

ICograph 4

Primary Market Targets

Susceptibility Levels:

Literate, middle-aged house-wives; suburban high-school seniors; the Beautiful People; stockbrokers — 52% — I

Grandparents — 27% — II

The illiterate — 21% — III

% of Population

Exposition

Background: The Popularity of the Soap Opera

Since the beginning days of radio, and into the present era of television, the soap opera has held top audience ratings; not only do millions of viewers tune in and listen to soap operas, but more money is spent advertising products on these shows than on any other type of show.

What is the appeal? The obvious answer, and the answer

with which MCA agrees, is that the soap opera is closest to the *real-life* situations of millions of individuals, only in the soap opera, unlike in real life, "the suffering and pain of the individual is openly exposed for all to appreciate." The appeal of soap operas is no less than the appeal of the human situation itself: love won and lost, sickness befalling the most healthy, unwanted babies, tragic accidents, fortunes made and then lost, small men in Big Society, lonely mothers and angry children, forgotten old people and alienated youth, etc. The "dramatization" of these events is the way we often envisage them ourselves. Everyone's life is, in some rather obvious ways, a "soap opera."

The Soap-Opera Viewer and Projection

The individuals who regularly view soap operas see themselves, oftentimes, as the hero or heroine in the script; they project themselves and their lives into the story. This type of projection is exceedingly common, and not peculiar to soap opera viewers: everyone, at some time or other, projects himself into a story — be it James Bond stories, *Jack and Jill* stories, Tarzan stories, or what have you.

MCA delved deeply into this phenomenon, and revealed that virtually all people have a desire to see themselves as the "hero" or "heroine" in some highly stylized script — and this is particularly true of the soap-opera viewer. This fact provides the basis for the initiation of the Personalized Soap-Opera Service.

MCA research disclosed that millions of individuals (based on a carefully selected sample) responded with great enthusiasm to the question, "How would you like to have the major events in your life made into *your very own soap-opera script?*" The most enthusiastic respondents were housewives, stockbrokers, teen-agers of both sexes, the "Beautiful People." Intellectuals emphatically denied having such desires, but objective criteria — their dress, conversation, and most recent writings — just as emphatically proved their susceptibility. Additional research provided further support for the hypothesis that the Personalized Soap-Opera Service would be a whopping market success.

The "Standard Script" Explained

MCA shows that there are several *Basic Life Tragedies* (BLT) shared by virtually everyone. For example, the marriage-child-divorce-inlaw-grandparent-sickness BLT is extremely common; another example is the working-girl-shacked-up-lousy-boyfriend-ran-out-and-left-me-married-for-money-lovers-on-the-side-inheritance-blackmail-attempted-suicide BLT. Each of these Basic Life Tragedies (there are 7 in all), or *Standard Scripts,* will be written by skilled soap-opera writers and then *computerized. Blank spaces* will be provided throughout each BLT so that the *specific details* of the life of the client may be included; e.g., the client's name, names of friends, relatives, acquaintances, places of importance, dates, times, etc. Each Standard Script will be *written in the same style* as those of the soap operas one sees on TV. These scripts will be highly melodramatic, emphasizing the major life-events of the client and being certain to *embellish* these events so as to highlight their *emotional com-*

ponent. Needless to say, the client will be written into the script so that he/she is always the *center* of attraction.

The Very Personal Script

The Service can arrange a *unique* script for the client, but the fee will be considerably higher than for the Standard Script. Many individuals, it is expected, will feel that their life is so special it cannot be adequately represented by any of the BLT's. In this case, in-depth interviews will be conducted by the Service staff and a very personal soap opera will be written for the client. The forthcoming innovations in "home" video tapes add an obvious, but expensive, spin-off.

The Staff

The staff should be carefully selected from the 3,212 writers who are currently employed, or have been employed, as soap-opera writers. Those writers selected, in addition to being able to write emotional scripts, should have the added ability of being able to *interview clients*, so that the most engrossing details will be "drawn out." There are no additional personnel needed for initiations of the Service, save for a core of typists, who have been "sworn to secrecy," to complete final personalized manuscripts.

CHAPTER SEVEN

Ex-Celebrity Service

Service

Ex-Celebrity Service

Function and Nature

A "home-delivery" entertainment service which: provides the "organized" public (formal organizations, public institutions, clubs, etc.) and the "unorganized" public (class reunions, bachelor parties, Bar Mitzvahs) with a great variety of inexpensive ex-celebrities to entertain them; provides employment to ex-celebrities.

Market Creation

The constant demand in the mass media for "new faces" has resulted in the "overnight creation" of celebrities and then the "dropping" of these people from the public eye: thus, the creation of *ex-celebrities*. MCA estimates there are currently 14,379 such individuals, and roughly 78% wish to perform for people if given the opportunity. Correspondingly, there is the universal need among organizations, institutions, etc., for entertainers who are not exorbitantly priced. The Ex-Celebrity Service, with its staff of "celebrity lovers," unites the "public" and the "ex-celebrities" for entertainment and profit. There is a very strong natural base for this Service, ensuring its immediate success with minimal effort. In a short time, a "stable of entertainers" could be ready and waiting (at no standby pay) to perform for the public which requests them).

ICograph 5

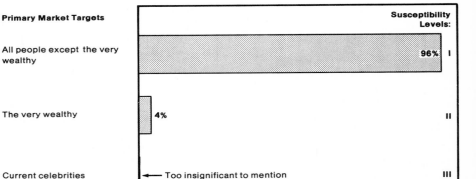

Exposition

The Universal Need for Entertainment

Every known culture, from the simplest to the most complex, has its celebrities or entertainers. In our society, it is predicted that by the year 2000 at least ⅓ of the population will be "in entertainment." All people, so far as anyone can tell, like to be amused from the earliest years of life: fathers "clown" for their infants while mothers "sing" — and the infant appears to love it (this is supported by the scientific evidence available). Elementary schools provide entertainment in the auditorium, and this continues throughout the educational process, oftentimes directly in the classroom.

As individuals grow older, they pay great sums of money to be entertained — and think nothing of it. A peculiar thing about the need for entertainment is that it seems to be satisfied most when *shared with others* — when "the group" sees a movie or watches a juggler or talks with a politician, the enjoyment is intensified. Parallel to the need to be entertained and perfect for MCA exploitation — is the desire to "know" someone famous, obviously motivated by a mass society increasingly faced with uncertainty and identity crises. In any case, people view the entertainment-celebrity complex as important and even necessary. The Ex-Celebrity Service is designed to bring famous entertainers to everyone's doorstep and thus satisfy the universal need for entertainment and recognition.

The Ex-Celebrities

The growth of mass media created a constant demand for "celebrities" of all sorts — and many such celebrities were, and are, "created overnight." Not surprisingly, just as quickly these celebrities "drop" from the media — to make room for "new" celebrities. This process has been going on now for just under two decades.

What has become of all those "dropped" celebrities? MCA compiled a list of people who at some point in the past two decades were defined as "media celebrities": 14,379 people are on that list, which includes show-biz people, politicians, athletes, authors, *ad IC*. Some of these people are now in private businesses, some are on the fringe of show biz (but mostly out of work), some are teachers, some are "loafers," and so on. MCA contacted 500 of these individuals, and of these, 462 have one thing in common: *they remember when* . . . and they still wish to "perform" for audiences if encouraged! Some expressed a desire to just talk with an audience, some to sing for people, some to tap-dance; in general, to "do their thing."

The "Group" Market

There are two basic kinds of groups, the "formal" and the "informal." The "organized public" (formal groups) consists of schools, women's clubs, prisons, mental institutions, and so on. Many of these groups, organizations, and institutions hire people to provide entertainment of one sort or another. And, MCA shows, they could be made to hire *more* if (a) there were more "interesting people" to hire; (b) the price of entertainment weren't so high; (c) the most basic MCA techniques were used to reinforce the average citizen's feeling of "being left out."

We showed a sample of the organized public a partial list (compiled by MCA) of ex-celebrities, and, as expected, the response was overwhelmingly enthusiastic: *once brought to memory*, the interest in the ex-celebrities is immediate. They can be wanted once the public feels *unimportant enough* because it doesn't *know anyone important*.

The "unorganized" or "general" public (informal groups) will be contacting the Ex-Celebrity Service once it is established, and will provide for enormous sales. Some examples of "informal get-togethers" which will utilize the Service are (1) class reunions; (2) bachelor parties; (3) block parties; (4) Bar Mitzvahs, weddings, wakes, etc.; (5) house-apartment parties (birthday, welcome-home, Halloween, "nothing-special" parties, etc.).

Each and any of the above assure IGP (Infinite Growth Potential) for the Service. It should be noted that the more people involved, the less the cost to any one of them! Thus, if 50 people were having a party, it would only cost each person $1 (assuming a $50/hr. standard fee) for an hour of singing by, say, Snooky Lansen. Or, for *multiple performances*, for $2 hr./person, those at the party could also have an hour of Jon Hall (*Ramar of the Jungle*) imitating ape calls.

Organizing the Ex-Celebrity Service

To start the E.C.S. it is only necessary to get together the ex-celebrities and the public in some efficient manner, negotiate fees and traveling arrangements, and profit from each arrangement. The easiest way to begin is to —

(1) compile a list of ex-celebrities with phone numbers, addresses, and brief biographies stressing "recognizable moments" (e.g., if the performer wore a costume which identified him, this should be pointed out);

(2) compile a list of organizations with addresses, chairmen's names, nature of organization, etc.;

(3) contact the ex-celebrities (this will require time, but

little capital) and tell them that (if they agree) their names will be on a *circulating list* with other ex-celebrities to be shown to organizations who desire entertainment, and

(4) the key step: show the list of ex-celebrities to the organizations, clubs, etc., around the country, and explain the nature of the list. The promotion material included in this material demonstrates that no one is anyone unless he knows someone (Shameless Factor) and suggests the possible loss of popularity and/or memberships (Threat) in the event of a negative response. In most instances (MCA test study showed 92%), *someone* on the list not only will be selected but also will be *excitedly demanded!* Once the celebrity is selected, the Service representative tells the client the *approximate* cost of the endeavor: e.g., standard pay, traveling costs, the Service's arrangement fee, etc. The decision is then left to the organizational representative and should present no difficulty. The celebrity selected is then contacted.

The chosen ex-celebrity is contacted by the Service, told the date for which he has been requested and any *particular* details (such as a request to sing an "old favorite"), and asked if he can appear; if he can appear, and it is a *standard assignment*, he receives a *standard fee* (see below: "Ex-Celebrity Pay Scale"), plus traveling expenses.

Upon arrival of the ex-celebrity, the Service collects the contracted fee, pays the ex-celebrity, and pays itself!

Staffing the Ex-Celebrity Service

A large staff is not needed, but all those on the staff must be "celebrity lovers," as so many people have to be contacted:

the staff must love the work. Ideally, the staff will consist of ex-celebrities, many of whom will know the ex-celebrities they are contacting. This situation will provide for immediate rapport, and increase the likelihood of the "ex-celebrity stable" growing in the future.

Some Examples of Test Runs

1. A chairman of a woman's club looked at our partial list. After passing such names as Charles Van Doren, Margaret Truman, Eddie Mayehoff, Betty White, Mr. Ed, Roberta Quinlan, Russell Arms, and Tony Marvin, she excitedly stopped at Jay Silverheels: "Tonto." "How marvelous it would be to have 'Tonto' chat with us at our annual meeting!" Interestingly enough, she did not previously plan to have an "entertainer" at the meeting — such is the *suggestive power* of the list!

2. A Golden-Age Club was to have a costume party, and when we arrived, they were in the process of deciding whom to invite as a "guest celebrity." When the list was presented, the name of Lyndon Johnson struck like thunder! "We want him — how much?!"

3. An athletic club became wildly enthusiastic at the words "Roger Bannister" and asked if he could be hired to run for them for an hour.

4. A sadist club thought it would be a great idea to have Guy Williams (Zorro) appear in full regalia.

Market Permanency

Any entertainment business is heavily dependent upon "general economic conditions," entertainment oftentimes being defined as a luxury. The Ex-Celebrity Service, likewise, will be affected by such conditions. But — and this must be emphasized — entertainment is a constant and is *always desired* — thus, the *product* (entertainment) is permanent and economic slumps have been *temporary* in the U.S. Should business be slow, however, it will be realized that the material (the entertainers) are on stand-by, free of charge, and thus the costs of upkeep of the Service are virtually nil. Should a "permanent" economic slump befall us, then it will be necessary for MCA to redefine entertainment as a *necessity*, and the costs of doing this will have to be weighed against estimated profits.

CHAPTER EIGHT

Statistical Normative Service

Service

Statistical Normative Service

Function and Nature

A computerized telephone information and/or in-person service to alleviate anxiety; *specify* what is moral, good, or right in diverse areas of human behavior; *define* what is moral, good, or right in ambiguous areas of human behavior; facilitate increased opportunism.

Market Creation

The Statistical Normative Service provides "instant" computerized information to people wanting to know how to act, or what to do, in given situations. The "other-directed" personality type (characteristic of the Great Middle Classes in our society) continually asks the question: *"What is expected of me?"* This question, formerly answered by tradition and the more familiar round of life characteristic of days gone by, leaves individuals in our fast-moving society anxiety-ridden, error-prone, and uncertain of themselves — in other words, perfect members of IC society. In response to this "What is expected of me?" syndrome, the Statistical Normative Service provides information, in *probability* form, to virtually any question relating to custom, morality, travel, costuming, dating behavior, and so on. In answering such questions, the Service not only alleviates general anxiety (its major function) but also encourages "one-upmanship" by providing general, instantaneous information and defines the nature of "new" behaviors.

ICograph 6

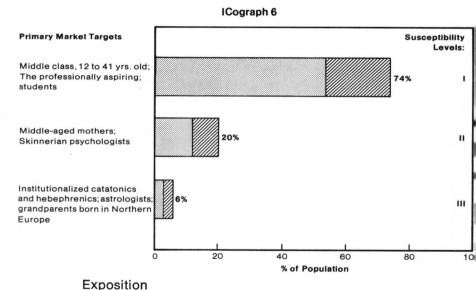

Exposition

Background and Basis

Almost two decades ago, David Riesman convincingly argued in *The Lonely Crowd* that a major shift in *character structure* had taken place in the United States population, as well as in other advanced industrial nations. The shift was from what he termed an "inner-directed" personality to an "other-directed" personality. Although there are some positive aspects to the "other-directed" type, the major characteristics are negative: (1) this personality is highly incapable of pursuing a goal, both in respect to means and ends; (2) this personality is highly incapable of defining for itself "what is *expected* of it." To answer this question, "What is expected of me?" the "other-directed" personality must look to *others* (usually peers) for the answer, and of course, these "others" are also looking to others for answers. The primary psychological characteristics of this personality are a craving for "acceptance" from others, and corresponding to this, a constant *anxiety* that acceptance will not be forthcoming. This human condition provides the basis for the Statistical Normative Service.

FUNCTIONS OF THE STATISTICAL NORMATIVE SERVICE

1. Alleviate Anxiety. Let us illustrate this with a common example. A family has just moved to a new neighborhood and is very conscious about "fitting in" with their neighbors. They especially want to get just the "right" kind of *furniture*. What kind of furniture should they buy? Modern? Traditional? Bohemian? Space age? Bordello? The wrong decision could mean "nonacceptance," and the family is thus suffering intense anxiety.

The Statistical Normative Service could easily answer the question, "What kind of furniture should I buy?" by specifying what % of people in the neighborhood described have what kind of furniture; also, the Service could answer questions for this family as regards acceptable methods of child rearing, automobiles, Easter, music, war toys, dog food, the Catholic Church, the Communists, etc.

2. *Specify and/or Define What Is Moral, Good, Right.* A common question is, "Do most people do this?" If the answer is *yes*, this is usually taken as a sign that what is done will also be "good," "moral," or "right." In short, the question of morality in our culture, for most people, is answered *quantitatively*: do *most* people do this or that? Thus, to answer questions of "goodness," or of "morality," people generally have a *statistical picture* in mind. How many people gamble? Is it moral to gamble? How many people believe in God? How many people masturbate? Questions such as these can either be answered *generally* — with reference to the society as a whole — or for a particular *subgroup* in society. For example, if one is only interested in data on one's *own* religious group, one might want the question of "belief in God" answered specifically for his group. For questions of a less clear-cut nature, the Statistical Normative Service could be of invaluable aid in actually *defining* what is moral when no actual evidence is available to draw upon.

3. *Increase Opportunism.* Many people wish to know what is expected of them in given situations to "gain the upper hand," "increase chances of success," etc. This is particularly common in two areas of behavior: business and sex. For example, a college male who wants to "score" with his date may feel he will be aided in his endeavor if the girl will smoke some marijuana. Would it offend his date if he offers her a marijuana cigarette? The Statistical Normative Service could easily answer this question. The male gives the S.N.S.

all the information about his date that he has: e.g., religion, economic class, physical features, education, age, etc. Information of this sort is easily answered in probabilistic terms. The answer could be that "87% of the girls similarly described have smoked marijuana, or they would like to try smoking if they had the opportunity."

A common example from the business world is as follows. A worker in a large firm has been offered a chance for promotion. He will be sent from New York, where he was born and has worked all his life, to Boise, Idaho, on a trial period as manager. While in Boise, he is expected to meet the company executives who have lived there all their lives. In New York he was constantly told that the guys in Boise are a bunch of "real characters." *What does this mean?* How do people in Boise act? "What is expected of me," the man may ask, "in the way of dress, jokes, cars, cigarettes, women, language, food habits, business mannerisms?" The Statistical Normative Service could quickly provide the client with some "general norms" about Boise and, second, specific information about the life-styles of his new colleagues.

Initiating the Statistical Normative Service

To initiate such a service, one would need the following: (1) an A-1361-TX computer which would be programmed in-depth with statistical information from almanacs, fact books, results of statistical surveys conducted by market researchers and public-opinion firms, statistical information compiled by social scientists in the course of their work; in addition would be information from argot manuals, cross-cultural files, newspapers and magazines, plus the wealth of knowledge from private and public organizations which have "study banks" on travel, dating, furnishing, customs, etc.; (2) programming specialists; (3) a small staff of researchers (at least in the beginning) to continually update statistical tables on areas of human behavior which are highly susceptible to change, such as fashion, waterfront language, political attitudes, etc.

Once the A-1361-TX computer was programmed, the rest would simply be a matter of providing clients who either called the Service or utilized it in person with the appropriate information. The fee for the Service would vary with the request or the difficulty of obtaining the answer.

CHAPTER NINE

Degree-Faking Service

Service

Degree-Faking Service

Function and Nature

An in-person, staff-client interaction, consulting-and-information service to provide "non-degreed" people with the know-how to pass themselves off as degree-holders so that they may more equally compete in the job market; contribute to an undermining of the "credentialed" society; provide psychologically stressed adults in "adult higher education" with an alternative to the formal educational system.

Market Creation

The "degree" from a college is considered necessary to get a "good job" and yet many people will never get the degree. The Degree-Faking Service is a response to this discrepancy. The Service will cater primarily to the millions of bright youngsters in our society who think they have been "left out." Since a degree usually does not actually aid one in the job one ultimately does, and since it is not "checked out" most of the time, it is concluded that the degree is primarily an informal device to "sift out" personality types. The analysis concluded by MCA states that to "get a good job" one must "come on" *as if* he had the degree — and this is primarily a matter of one learning the appropriate words, phrases, and mannerisms typical of collegiate reality. Providing such a vocabulary and life-style and the confidence to use it casually is the primary function of the D.F.S. In addition to youth, MCA will focus on adults currently in night schools who are desperately looking for a way out. These frustrated individuals will be more than willing to present themselves as "other than they are," once informed of the essentially false nature of the society in which they live.

ICograph 7

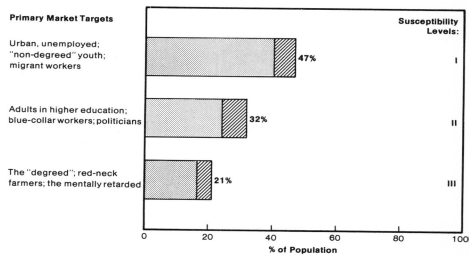

Primary Market Targets

Susceptibility Levels:

Urban, unemployed; "non-degreed" youth; migrant workers — 47% — I

Adults in higher education; blue-collar workers; politicians — 32% — II

The "degreed"; red-neck farmers; the mentally retarded — 21% — III

0   20   40   60   80   100

% of Population

Exposition

Jobs and Degrees

"To get a good job, get a good education." This National Slogan makes it appear as if there were an actual relationship between the "job" and the "education"; it also implies that the only kind of education that is worth anything is the kind you get in "schools" (it is admitted "off the cuff," however, that there are other kinds of education). The fact is that a "good (formal) education" is *irrelevant* to most jobs — and especially most "good" jobs. The slogan really means: *only certain kinds of people* go to schools of higher learning — and these people are to be rewarded with the good jobs. As proof that an education has been had, there is the *degree:* if the individual has left school 1 (one) day before receiving the degree, *he never attended!* This is the nature of a *credential-oriented* society.

More than anything else, the degree tells the prospective employer about the job-seeker's ability to "get along" in a bureaucratic setting: after all, he never would have made it through if he were an *emotional* being, punching teachers, cursing, breaking property. The employer-to-be looks at the person who "has the degree" and says: "Here, at least, is a human being capable of rational *control.*"

Untraining the Degree-Holder

That the degree has little relationship to the job is indicated by the fact that in many cases an employer has to "untrain" a degree-holder and then "retrain" him to do the

job "the company's way." Because this is costly, there is a
tendency for employers to hire degree-holders, but with a degree in a *different* area from the one in which the job is to be
held; this saves the employer the time and cost of "untraining" the new job-holder.

Presentation of Self

How does an employer know if an individual *actually* has
a degree? One would think that with all the emphasis on degrees in our society, the employer would *check* to see if the
job-seeker had his degree. But, MCA shows that for *all* employers, 84% of the time there is *no* check *if* the job-seeker
presents himself as a degree-holder! The national slogan
should read, then, "To get a good job, come on like you
have a degree — even if you don't!"

COMING ON AS A DEGREE-HOLDER: Degree-holders (actual) have
gone through college and have acquired the *collegiate vocabulary* (if nothing else). Such a vocabulary *defines* one as
a member of that reality: the collegiate reality. Thus, by
using the *right words* and *right phrases, anyone* can define
himself as a degree-holder. For example, the individual who
can casually toss about such words as "cumulative average,"
"intersession," "visiting professor," "registrar." "School of
Liberal Arts," "lab," etc., is, for all intents and purposes, a
member of the collegiate reality.

If an individual, then, can acquire the *confidence* to portray himself comfortably as a degree-holder, the task is
won (in 84% of the cases). And if there is a checkup? This
simply means — *it is time to try again!*

The Youth Market

11.3 million bright youngsters in our society between the ages of 17 and 26 will never get to college and thus will never get a degree and thus will never get a "good job." At least this is the analysis *prior* to the existence of the Degree-Faking Service. These people will be heavy users of the D.F.S. once they are informed of it, gain confidence in it, and are made to accept it as a fast solution to their job problems. MCA shows that such youth (93%) do not personally know degree-holders, and thus will be entirely dependent on the D.F.S.

Staffing the Degree-Faking Service

Ideally, the staff of the D.F.S. will have knowledge of both the collegiate reality and the *job-market reality*: this way the gap is bridged by the staff. Thus, it would be wise to utilize people who have worked, e.g., in employment agencies, as psychological testers for job applicants in business, or in personnel departments. Such individuals should be chosen for their particular *dislike* of the credentialing system, as this will assure a *guilt-free attitude*; if this is not so, the staff may ultimately begin to feel they are "cheating the system," and their performance will be less than maximal.

Finally, in addition to their being familiar with the collegiate and job-market realities, it would be best if the staff were also *minority-group* members, particularly *nonwhite*. Thus, a staff member who (1) holds a B.A. degree; (2) previously worked as a job personnel consultant; (3) hates the system; (4) is Puerto Rican, Black, Indian, or Chicano would be *perfect*. MCA indicates there are roughly 11,500 people with these or similar characteristics and qualifications.

The Service in Action

A black high-school dropout, 19 years old, comes to the D.F.S. stating he wants to get a "good job." He is asked his "area of interest," and this is discussed. Some area *must be decided upon*, because the D.F.S. will "Degreeify" the client in a *totally unrelated area*: this will minimize conflict and is consistent with the trend as explained above (*see* "untraining the Degree-Holder"). The important thing is that he be able to portray himself as *a* (any) degree-holder.

The client and "faking consultant" decide upon the degree area, say Sociology, and the client is handed a *standard list* of sociological jargon, consisting of such commonly used terms as "reification," "role," "socialization," "Parsons," "technological adaptation," "Mental Health Foundation," "creaming the poor," etc. It doesn't matter if the client understands these terms in any *depth*, for it is not likely that the employer — or bona fide degree-holders, for that matter — will understand them either. Thus, short definitions and/or identifications will be adequate, to be stated ambiguously (this will increase credibility).

The client is assigned a college, and in addition to the *standard list*, is given a *list of faculty members* in that department. In a short while he will feel comfortable saying, "Oh, yes, Professor Blum was my informal adviser during the Spring Semester; we worked together on a critique of the Plowitz Theory as interpreted by Sjoberg and young Myrdal."

When such words and phrases are comfortably part of the client's reality, he is then given a brief lesson in the "job interview situation" which is simulated by the D.F.S. If the D.F.S. staff member can suggest a possible job, and is familiar with the interviewer, then this, of course, greatly increases the probability of the client's getting the job (but getting jobs for clients, it is understood, is *not* the function of the D.F.S.).

When it is decided by both client and staff member that the client is able to present himself convincingly as a degree-holder, the "session" is completed.

Market Permanency

The number of people who *now* will never get a degree guarantees the long-run existence and success of this Service, and this number is growing by leaps and bounds as the system is proving itself incapable of absorbing large numbers of its citizens into the school-job-success-retirement complex. The only way this Service will become obsolete is if degrees are no longer used as primary proof of one's intelligence, or ability, or desire to do a good job. But the trend appears to be in the *opposite* direction.

Students in the Dark

At present there are 8 million adults attempting to acquire "higher degrees" either by mail or by personally attending "night school." These people are generally frustrated and are only going to school to get their degree. MCA techniques can convince these foolish individuals that they are wasting their time. The D.F.S. should be presented as a *sensible alternative* to the demeaning and tortuous process of "adult higher education." Such people will generally be *highly* susceptible to the D.F.S., as most are bored, frustrated, and/or totally alienated with their present situation.

An Added Note on Creating the D.F.S. Market

MCA techniques will focus upon redefining "false presentation of self" as a respectable activity. Throughout the D.F.S. training program, the staff will subtly indicate the "respected" societal members who are fakes, liars, cheats, and imposters — and will particularly stress those individuals who *admit* to being so. Given the fact that most individuals realize, even if only subconsciously, that this society is premised upon false values, there will be little difficulty in creating the appropriate image — and thus market — for the Degree-Faking Service.

CHAPTER TEN

Patriotic Society

Service

Patriotic Society

Function and Nature

A chain of vacation resorts catering to Liberal, Conservative, and extreme Right-Wing Patriots which enables them to vacation with others of like mind and to express their patriotic consciousness freely in a sympathetic environment; reinforces patriotic beliefs among the morally confused.

Market Creation

Detailed research shows that politically conscious individuals — be they liberals, conservatives, or right-wingers — find it difficult to "be themselves" because of the tensions which exist in our society. Many people today seek like-minded individuals with and to whom they can comfortably and unabashedly express their political views without meeting resistance. MCA shows that this desire is particularly strong when one has a lot of "free time" — such as on vacations and holidays. The Patriotic Society, a chain of vacation resorts, is designed to cater to these politically conscious individuals by providing them with total environments — people, nature, food, music, lecture halls, and so on — in which to relax and freely express their political views. Careful screening of political types guarantees liberal, conservative, and right-wing "resort homogeneity."

ICograph 8

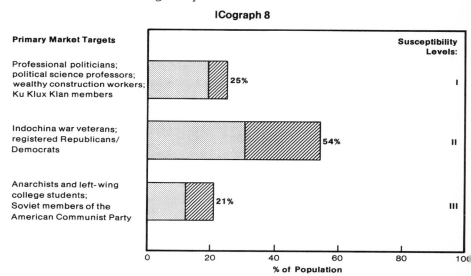

Primary Market Targets

Susceptibility Levels:

Professional politicians; political science professors; wealthy construction workers; Ku Klux Klan members — 25% — I

Indochina war veterans; registered Republicans/ Democrats — 54% — II

Anarchists and left-wing college students; Soviet members of the American Communist Party — 21% — III

0   20   40   60   80   100

% of Population

Exposition

Background

In any democratic nation, it is expected that political conflicts will create *national* tensions. Needless to say, this sometimes stimulates considerable debate, demonstration, legal constitutional assaults, and demagogy.

Today, in America, the individual also lives in a paradoxical world of compromise designed to prevent either solutions or dangerous hostility. This has sometimes been referred to as the "American Way." The paradox is this: Seeking to be honest and justly to express his views, the individual forced to compromise his tone, his information, and his integrity feels constant hypocrisy, a condition resulting in ill health, which occasionally takes its mental toll. The issue can perhaps be exemplified this way: *How Can an American Fascist Be Himself?* Or: How can a middle-of-the-road individual (sometimes known as a Liberal) salute his flag and at the same time propose social reform that might upset the bulk of the American population?

The Patriotic Society as a Response to the Paradox

The Patriotic Society is designed to allow these tormented individuals to *be themselves* in an atmosphere of patriotic homogeneity. Liberal with Liberal. Conservative with Conservative. Fascist with Fascist. The Service provides a vacation for all screened and approved applicants which guarantees them that they can say, feel, and do what they please away from any form of social or political conflict. The Service also allows those individuals who feel some moral confusion (doubtless from the increasing amount of hostile political exchange) to reinforce their wavering political contentions. These individuals will no doubt be among the Liberal vacationers.

Service Facilities and Staff

Three vacation resorts in "desolate nature playgrounds" will accommodate the three groups of vacationers. The staff needed to operate the service will be a research-and-testing team stationed at the PS Headquarters (*see* section below), management teams, and carefully chosen waiters, motion-picture-camera operators, musicians, former army, navy, air force, coast guard, and marine personnel, munition specialists, social historians, macro-sociologists, Friedmanesque economists, and a multitude of professional, military, and academic personnel (on a call, stand-by basis). Staff members for the three vacation resorts will be carefully screened to match the guests politically.

Service Utilization: Contact, Screening, and Referral

To make an appointment for a vacation, the client calls the Service at least one month in advance. This will allow the research team to make a comprehensive security check on the client to ensure vacation-resort homogeneity. When the client comes to the Service, a battery of psychological tests will be given and a quick computer analysis of the information made. *The nature of the client's political affiliation will be established*, and the client will be referred to one of the three resorts. If there is any disagreement between client and Service referral judgment, an additional series of tests will be given. Decision of the Service will be final (to protect vacationers against unqualified lay opinion).

The Three Resorts

LIBERAL RESORT. The atmosphere here will reflect the *pluralistic spirit* of modern American Liberalism. Representing the *functional unity* of America, portraits of racial and ethnic heroes will be proudly displayed. For example, Black heroes should include Jackie Robinson, Roosevelt Greer, and Wilt Chamberlain. Jewish heroes *must* include Arthur Goldberg, comedian Sam Levenson, "Gambling Czar" Howard Samuels, and celebrity Georgie Jessel.

Presidential heroes might include Roosevelt, Truman, and Johnson. Flags of the many ethnic "nations" will abound throughout the resort. On *all* bathrooms, the sign *INTE-GRATED* will appear, and *information booths* on environmental protection will be found near all tennis courts. Facilities will include convention halls, lecture rooms, theaters (where documentaries will be shown on the social improvements made during the New Deal, the Fair Deal, the New Frontier, and the Great Society), library space featuring lectures on the works of Montaigne, Jack Newfield, and Jean-Jacques Rousseau (on the library door will be a plaque commemorating the *now famous* "Man is born free and everywhere he is in chains"), a Winston Churchill Tomb, and a Shock Theater showing movies of disadvantaged children in rural America.

1. Activities. For educational purposes, social scientists will present lecture series on the *plight* of the American Indian, Black, Mexican, Chinese, Jew, Pole, Russian, Puerto Rican, and Lebanese (*ad* IC). In addition, guest speakers will be invited to insult liberal vacationers.

Nightly sing-songs, camp-outs, wienie-marshmallow roasts, and poetry readings will provide evening entertainment. Integrated bowling and billiards will be provided for males. For the avant-garde, sexual games such as Red Light-Green Light and Spin the Bottle will be "sanctioned" (in the liberal spirit).

2. Liberal Resort Etiquette. Anyone can participate in any activity as long as he is qualified to do so. For example, according to etiquette, it would be considered extremely discourteous if a Black man, not educated in sociology, contradicted an urban specialist while he was making a public presentation illustrating his thesis that Blacks "remain at the bottom of the totem pole because they have inadequate family structure." Such action could be defined as *radical*, and the "deviant" might be asked to leave the resort. The reasoning for such a ruling would be according to this traditional liberal "rule of thumb": *There are appropriate measures that can be taken through appropriate channels.*

3. The Confused Liberal: Latency. MCA estimates that there are presently 22 million confused liberals. This simply means that although these individuals are deeply immersed in the Liberal Tradition, they find themselves *sometimes* wondering about their political incentives concerning minority group members. It is primarily for these individuals that social scientists with the aid of motion pictures will present *optimistic social reform statistics.* Reinforced and no longer suffering, these men and women will go forth and work toward a better society!

CONSERVATIVE RESORT. The decor at this resort will be *somber.* The atmosphere, reflecting the aura of the "debating" and "thinking" conservative, will be extremely conducive for polemic construction against the Liberal Mind. Painted in half-tone colors, and lacking outlandish emotional displays of nationalistic megalomania, the resort will be highly suitable to the value-neutral and traditional scholar-writer.

1. Activities. Much of the resort activity will center on well-disciplined debates, panel discussions on the stupidity of liberals, charades, and Ping-Pong. Instructional classes on the *debating arts* such as pantomime, diction, and mimicry will be available. For the nonintellectual, sports events such as marbles, wrestling, and lawn-bowling will be provided.

2. *Conservative Resort Etiquette*. Syntax must exclude the use of four-letter words. If guilty of such a violation, the "deviant" will be presumed to be a liberal who has infiltrated and will be efficiently "removed."

RIGHT-WING EXTREMIST RESORT. This resort will resemble a military encampment with Service "Generals" in military uniforms patrolling the grounds at all hours. Decor will include portraits *in all buildings* of persons such as Shirley Temple Black, Mussolini, Richard Nixon, and Tony Boyardo.

1. *Right-Wing Military Scenarios*. The P.S. will provide a number of miltiary, vigilante, and police scenarios. Possible systems include simulated national-guard "kills," police riot participation, and runaway-slave hunts.

2. *Other Activities*. MCA has shown that out of 2,507 extremists interviewed, 97% declared that singing was an important extremist attribute. Such songs as "God Bless America," "The Hanging Tree," and "The Star-Spangled Banner" led the list of favorites. Such an activity will be a feature of this resort, possibly as a Sing-a-Long Program. In the resort gymnasium, the client may use the great variety of *ethnic and racial dummies* for punching practice (the "Jew," the "Jap," and the "Polack" will be among the most greatly used).

3. *Right-Wing Extremist Resort Etiquette. All male vacationers will have their hair closely cropped (¼ inch) or com-*

pletely shaven. Women will wear their hair short and neatly tied at all times. All violators will be suspected of being infiltrating conservatives or liberals.

The Lifetime Patriotic Program

If a client has been accredited by the Service and has gone on at least *three* vacations to *one* resort, he will qualify for retirement benefits (a lifetime stay) enabling him to be forever free of political conflict and irritation.

Switching Political Categories

The Patriotic Society will have extremely rigid qualifications for mobility from one political category to another (e.g., MCA estimates that switches from Liberal to Conservative will occur at a rate of 13% a year, thus placing a burden on the Conservative Resort). Requirements for switching will be (1) a thorough psychological examination; (2) a loyalty oath and signature of a liability clause to protect the Service from infiltration (*see* below "Possible Infiltration"); and (3) four letters of recommendation from *established* Service clientele. In addition, all children of clients will be presumed to have similar political dispositions unless they can show otherwise (meeting above requirements for switching).

Possible Infiltration

If infiltration should occur, the Service must protect itself. This can easily be done by having the client sign a Liability Clause stating that he will be responsible for all damage suits should he be involved in an incident damaging to the Society.

CHAPTER ELEVEN

VOG: Voices of God

Service

Voices of God (VOG)

Function and Nature

An in-person multifunctional religious service to provide for personalized scenarios and environments in which religious expression can be fulfilled; offer religious sanctioning for baptisms, Bar Mitzvahs, weddings, etc., to excommunicants and other religious outcasts; provide for general amusement within a religious context; provide employment for defrocked clergy.

Market Creation

Religion, like other traditional institutions which no longer satisfy the needs of millions of Americans, is in a state of rapid change. Highly characteristic of this change is that millions of individuals are being viewed, or view themselves, as "outcasts" from traditional religious institutions. These people, *wanting religious sanctioning and comfort,* cannot obtain these from established institutions. Also obvious is the rash of clergy who no longer unquestionably accept their traditions; many such clergy have been defrocked by their superiors and are now looking for employment. Voices of God (VOG), the alternative to traditional religion, takes the utmost care to create very carefully the exact experience, as specified by the "outcast" client, required for religious observances in an atmosphere of respectful dignity. The Service, *denying no one*, refuses no form of religious request (e.g., witchcraft) and accommodates even the most macabre indulgence in private religious fantasy.

ICograph 9

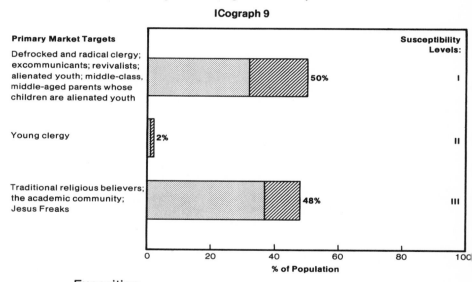

Exposition

Background

Man's relationship to Creation has changed. No longer is there the idea of THE CREATOR (God) and THE CREATED (man), but now man also is a Creator who creates machines which in turn create other machines. So confusing and profound is this revolutionary drama that modern man, no longer magnetized to an outdated form of spiritualism, faces the task of completely reevaluating his quest for Being. As the spiritual revolution grows, coupled with the traumas of economic strife, more and more individuals find themselves without a place to turn for sanctified religious comfort. Seeking new forms of religious experience and the dignity that befits their individuality and freedom of expression, they turn to innovations, to prophets of the future, and to experiments of the mind. Voices of God, (VOG) is designed to fill the spiritual void created by this GREAT PERIOD OF TRANSITION.

Staffing the Service

Needed are defrocked priests and other Men of God who have lost faith in the prejudices of the past; skilled communications and photographic technicians; sociology-of-religion research specialists; Laingian psychiatrists; "confessionists" (who take case histories); guidance counselors; light-show artists knowledgeable in psychedelia; and electrical engineers. In addition, management personnel must include telephone order clerks, credit analysts, and a full legal staff. Auxiliary personnel will include professional mourners, "Best Men" (for weddings), pallbearers, flower porters, adept "role simulators" (e.g., a scenario might call for someone to "play" the Pope expertly for a deathbed scene), and "moonlighting" clergymen.

Facilities

Most VOG activities will be provided for at a Service Plaza. For example, weddings and all religious observances will be carried out as specified by the client in appropriate chambers (e.g., crypts and caverns), and burial services may be performed at the Plaza's own cemetery (*see* below, The Land of VOG). If, however, the client wishes a religious service rendered at his own home, the Service can easily arrange for this.

Using VOG

To have a personalized religious experience, a client may either phone the Service or visit to make an appointment. The client can either specify exactly what he wants, or, if undecided, he can be referred to the Service's counseling and psychiatric unit, where his confusion will be analyzed and a suggestion made. For example, MCA files reveal that a reputed Mafia chieftain, Reggie ("The Savage") Garafola — religious, devoted, just released from San Quentin — feels that he is being harassed by the FBI. His desire is simple: he knows that he no longer can go to his church on Mulberry Street for salvation without *invasion of privacy*. What "The Savage" requires is a private "prayer" plaza — which VOG will provide. In addition, the Service could suggest that the prayer plaza be photoflooded with pictures of Reggie's favorite saint. If desired, a mute Service priest could be present at the confessional.

Services Offered: Some Examples

The Voices Of God offers infinite scenarios, and its list of already established services could grow endlessly, subject to the imagination of the clients. For example, weddings could be given in the Plaza chapel, complete with photo-flooded three-dimensional environments (e.g., an ocean, a "Vatican," a rock festival, or a satanic cult wedding could be photographically created according to client specification). Some other examples are the following. *Sickness visitations:* a Service priest could be hired to visit a client's dying mother in the hospital (who had been excommunicated from her church) without her knowing that the priest was not "officially" sanctioned to perform Last Rites. In addition, if a Catholic man on his deathbed cried out for the Pope, the family could ask the Service to send a "visitation Pope."

The Land of VOG

VOG will provide a vacation-resort complex, including a religious amusement park complete with a "Tunnel of God," designed for those who feel that for many years religion has "been no fun." MCA has shown that 57% of those who are presently ready to discard traditional beliefs have become bored to tears of repetitious services and speeches. The Land of VOG, "where religion is fun," will be operated exactly like any vacation spot. For example, for the "daring," *the Angel Bar*, serving drinks such as the Mosque, the Catholic-a-Rum-Rum, the Greek-O, and the Tomb, provided by beautiful women in angel robes, will allow for pleasant rest. In the amusement park area, a ride such as *Death in Hell* could carry the tiny car and its occupants into the depths of the earth, complete with "the Devil's Nest," and for the skybound, the *Heaven Tree* will carry the occupants of a glass ball higher and higher into a giant ceiling of melted marshmallows. Along with these amusements, if requested, religious services such as burials would be performed by the defrocked clergy.

CHAPTER TWELVE

Anonymous Identity Bracelet

Product

"Anonymous" Identity Bracelet

Function and Nature

A fashion bracelet designed to allow individuals publicly to announce the personal "lack of identity" in our society; provide a "sense of community" among those who define themselves as anonymous; allow the individual to express political protest *fashionably*; give rich hippies another way to spend money on novelty.

Market Creation

The traditional identity bracelet has witnessed a loss of overall sales because of the "identity crisis" in the U.S. The fault lies not with the bracelet itself, but with the idea of having one's name or initials on the bracelet: this is because so many people feel they have "no identity" in our mass society. Thus, by inscribing the word "anonymous" on the bracelet, the entrepreneur can reactivate interest in this fashion item and at the same time cater to the demand for creative ways of registering protest in this society. For younger people, MCA will focus on the *protest* nature of the bracelet, and for older, middle-aged people, MCA will focus on the *bracelet* itself and underplay the protest. In both instances, however, the *anonymity* aspect will be heavily emphasized. It will not be difficult to create and supply this bracelet to an eagerly awaiting market, but this must be done *quickly* (to avoid competition) if the entrepreneur is not presently in the business of manufacturing bracelets.

Exposition

The Problem of Identification

For several years, the I.D. (identification) bracelet had great sales success, which has declined of late. The sales problem is not with the *bracelet* itself, but with the idea of "identification."

Many people today are reluctant to wear their name on the bracelet because they are undergoing an *identity crisis*, feeling as if they have *no identity*. Thus, MCA concludes that there are many people who desire to wear an I.D. Bracelet but who, at the same time, would feel dishonest, foolish, etc., wearing their name on it, since they feel they have "no identity" and thus nothing (theoretically) to put on the bracelet.

Reidentifying the Identity Bracelet

The problem for MCA was simply how to utilize the *bracelet* and yet redefine it to meet contemporary needs!

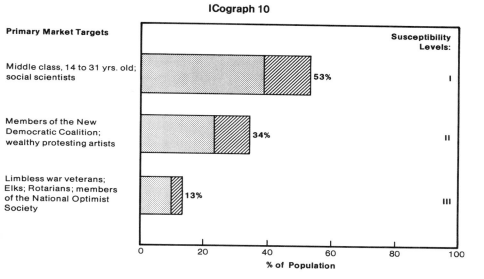

ICograph 10

The answer: engrave the word "anonymous" on the "identification bracelet." Not only will the Anonymous I.D. (A.I.D.) satisfy an obvious psychological need deriving from a sense of "aloneness" and "alienation" which plagues about 74% of the population; it will also serve to create the opposite of this: a sense of *community* among all those who wear the bracelet. Thus through *negating* one's original identity one creates a *new* identity. This is known as the "Bracelet Dialectic."

Because of the nature of the A.I.D., it is easy to define it not *only* as a fashion piece, not *only* as a *personal* statement, but as a statement of *public protest*. This is the basis for the creation of a market centering upon a political vortex.

The Market

Marketing will focus on white adolescents between the ages of 14 and 31, particularly in the middle class. Many such people already have I.D. bracelets, at home in their drawers, and thus will be reluctant to buy a new one — *unless* the anonymity-political aspect is promoted as opposed to the bracelet aspect.

A second source of primary sales will be the middle-aged. Middle-aged (white, middle-class) people will be reluctant to buy a political-protest item, but will buy jewelry, and will buy "novelty." Thus, MCA campaigns will stress the nonprotest aspect of the *bracelet* — but still stress the idea of *anonymity* (which does correlate with the middle-aged individual's psychological state). Fewer sales can be expected here than from among the youth, but will still contribute significantly to overall sales volume.

Geographical Note

Attention should be focused in large cities and college campuses, as these are places where feelings of anonymity are greatest and where politically conscious youth are most heavily concentrated. Small towns should be avoided initially, and only *after* the product has become a national success should the A.I.D. be imported as a "novelty item."

Market Permanency

Unless the entrepreneur is willing to go all out with MCA, or will be content with a "settling" market, the A.I.D. will *not* have lasting permanency on a large scale, and is intended, in fact, as an *IC-Quickie*. Need-creation, promotion, distribution, and manufacture will have to be done swiftly and in almost total secrecy to avoid competition from established I.D. bracelet manufacturers. If, however, the latter initiates this product, the problems are inconsequential.

CHAPTER THIRTEEN

Death Simulation Service

Service

Death Simulation Service

Function and Nature

An in-person, individualized therapeutic and/or "adventure" service, based upon principles of the controlled experiment, to provide for controlled near-death experiences in an age of increasing curiosity about death, increased numbers of suicides, and increased numbers of attempted suicides; allow for the exchange of information among those who have previously almost died; allow for individual psychological therapy centering on the death experience; allow the adventuresome the opportunity to "toy with death."

Market Creation

Mounting statistical evidence and suicide theory both indicate that people are taking their lives into their own hands at an alarming rate owing to alienation, frustration, boredom, and the recently emerging "romantic" view of death held by some of the young. Though there is no way to prevent this by law (it is already illegal to kill yourself), there is a way to *control* the death experience. The Death Simulation Service serves those individuals who wish to "experiment with death" — by any means of their own choosing. Under scientific conditions, the Service provides for a "near-death" experience as specified by the client; the staff, both laymen ("experts in death") and professionals (psychiatrists and physicians) supervise every near-death experience to see to it that an actual death does not occur. The Service will ensure that whatever the client recommends is provided down to the last detail, such as a specific-caliber bullet with which he is (supposedly) shot, a specific disease with which he is (allegedly) injected, a specified number of feet of water to drown in, a particular brand of acid to be saturated in, and so on. Because of the obvious potential dangers in operating a business such as this, the clients will, of necessity, be obliged to sign the Death Contract (which extricates the Service of responsibility) prior to the near-death experience. The Death Simulation Service is easily exportable, especially to capitalist and Protestant nations — where suicide rates tend to be highest.

Exposition

Background: Straight Facts on Suicide and Attempted Suicide

In the past decade the rate of suicide has slightly increased in the United States to its present 11.0 per 100,000 in the

ICograph 11

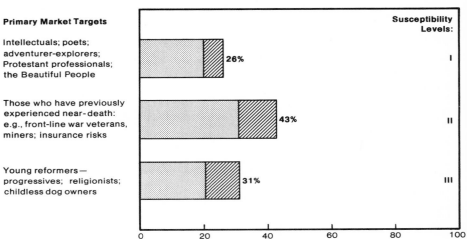

population. What is much more striking than this, however, is the rate of *attempted suicides*. This rate is estimated to be 6 to 10 times that of actual suicides. Latest figures for England and Wales, for example, which are estimated to be very similar to those of the U.S., indicate that there are between 30,000 and 40,000 attempted suicides per year. These figures are high and rising, and if theories are correct, they may be expected to increase still further. To cite just two major theories, Freud postulated that as "civilization" increased, there would be an increasing tendency by Man to turn his aggressions inward. Such turning of aggression inward is, in fact, one of the most widely accepted definitions of suicide. Durkheim, in his discussion of suicide, predicted that during rapid periods of social change there would be a lapse of normative controls, and this he related strongly to, what he termed, anomic suicide. What is highly significant in both of these theories is that the salient conditions leading to higher rates of both suicide and attempted suicide are *intensifying*.

Thinking the Unthinkable

In addition to the above factors, there is a general and increasing trend in our society for Man to "think about the unthinkable." Although it has been suggested that Man cannot fully conceive of his own death, mounting evidence suggests that this may no longer be the case. Many youths today see death as "romantic," and "challenging death" offers an alternative to a programmed life. It seems that Man's curiosity has exceeded all traditional boundaries. He is seriously considering what it might be like to die, and he is experimenting with this experience.

Although it is true that such experimentation is both harmful to the individual and his society, we believe there is no way to stop it at the moment. We do believe, however, that there is a way to *control* it. What we are here about to suggest, then, is the scientific application of the controlled experiment on an aspect of human behavior which, Goethe said, "demands the sympathy of every man, and in every age must be dealt with anew."

Functions of the Death Simulation Service

To this date, no ingenuity has been shown by businessmen to create a Service which would (1) give those individuals who are thinking of killing themselves the opportunity, under controlled conditions, to know what it would feel like to *almost die* (MCA believes that this is the only way to cut down on the rate of attempted suicides, many of which result in actual death); (2) provide a place for individuals to talk about their attempted suicides or close calls with death.

The Near-Death Experience

The Death Simulation Service, which will be staffed with "experts in death" (individuals who have almost died, understand death deeply, and desire to aid others in coming to grips with death), psychiatrists, and physicians, will be designed to cater to *individual preferences* in methods of dying. MCA shows that for those who seriously wish to die, the Service, to be maximally successful, must come as close to approximating *real death* as possible — and not merely provide "harmless simulation." For example, if the individual in question wanted to know what it would be like to drown, the Death Simulation Service would provide this experience for him/her *under controlled conditions* so as to assure that death would not actually result: the client would come as close to actually drowning as possible before being hauled out of the water and treated. This, hopefully, would satisfy the curiosity of the death-seeker, and thus enable him to live out his life in a more fulfilling manner than he otherwise might have done. Any individual preference could be satisfied easily, ranging from shooting, to fires, to being hit by a train, to overdoses of pills, to smothering, etc. And, in each instance, only a near-death would occur.

Following the Near-Death Experience

Following the near-death experience, the entire episode could be discussed with other clients of the D.S.S. In this way, *social support* would be afforded the attempted suicides, in much the same way that this principle works with AA and other organizations dealing with disturbed members in our society (*see* "Honesty Anonymous Service").

Finally, it should be mentioned that this Service could also cater to those individuals who have *already had* a close call with death — either through an attempted suicide or by a car accident, battles with sickness, etc. (MCA estimate — 27 million such people) — but who have no one with whom to talk over these experiences. The individuals would merely apply to the "conversational division" of the D.S.S., and in the enthusiastic presence of other "near-deathees," relate every minute detail of their close calls with death.

Staffing the D.S.S.

In our society, roughly 8.4 million people have attempted suicide by one means or another, at one time or another; these individuals are potentially "experts in death." Many of these individuals have "died" and have a deep understanding of the near-death experience. They will be invaluable as part of the staff of the D.S.S.

In recruiting these individuals it will be wise to focus on the *variety* of attempted suicides, as this will allow the Service the widest latitude in satisfying individual near-death experiences as requested by clients. These experts will "guide" the client on his near-death "trip," in addition to providing post-near-death verbal therapy. This will be a first step, before the client arrives at the "conversational division" of the D.S.S., in which only present "near deathees" discuss their experiences.

The D.S.S. will also staff certified psychiatrists and physicians who have focused their careers specifically on death, and who can provide for compassionate understanding in treating the client before and after the near-death experience. A physician or staff of physicians will have to be present at all times to treat those suffering from injury, such as from an arrow wound, or to officially declare an individual dead should the near-death experience go "overboard," or should the client die of fright during the near-death experience.

Psychiatrists also, needless to say, will be necessary at all times, since many individuals can be expected to go mad during the experience and remain that way for an unpredictable amount of time. The psychiatrist and "expert in death" will be needed to bring the individual back to reality, if possible. As this is generally an unpleasant experience for all concerned, pre-psychotics will not, if detected, be permitted to be clients.

The D.S.S. Contract

The Service cannot be responsible for actual deaths. Thus, the client will literally have to sign his life away. The exact details are to be specified in the Death Simulation Contract to be signed by all clients!

CHAPTER FOURTEEN

Infamous Genealogy Service

Service

Infamous Genealogy Service

Function and Nature

An in-person genealogy service to aid children of all ages in fighting the "generation war" against parents by providing them with "negative" information about family members both living and dead; provide youth with *positive* family identifications by stressing "black sheep," misfits, outcasts, and rebels; provide information which undermines false respectability in a hypocritical society; facilitate the unleashing of repressed hostilities against family members, and, especially among the middle-aged, to satisfy their desire to feel guilty.

Market Creation

The intrafamilial "generation war," and the lack of identification that youths have with "respectable" family members provide the basis for a service to discredit the family and simultaneously to provide positive identifications for youth.

This requires, in part, that family members such as horse thieves, pimps, necrophiliacs, gunrunners, etc. — who stud every family tree — be clearly identified. The infamous Genealogy Service provides such information about *specific individuals* as well as *general family* infamous genealogies. Organization of the Service is nonproblematic, as it is structurally similar to the already existent genealogy services, with which the entrepreneur can easily familiarize himself. Since this Service is dependent upon the generation war, should the war show signs of easing up, *artificial conflict* via MCA methods and techniques can easily be induced.

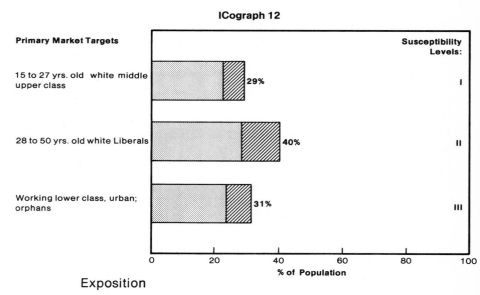

ICograph 12

Exposition

Background: The "Generation War"

In many parts of the United States the generations are at "war." Most generally, those in combat are of the same family. Children charge parents with "dishonesty," "hypocrisy," deception"; they insist that it's time to "reveal," "disclose," "tell it like it is." Simultaneous with this is the *lack of identification* that many children have with the "upright" members of the family: this is a time when primary identifications of youth are directed at rebels, outcasts, misfits.

These factors, combined with the great interest in genealogy in this society, provide the basis for the Infamous Genealogy Service (I.G.S.).

The Need to Discredit the Family

The I.G.S. will directly aid the many children today who wish to "discredit" their families. Such children, alienated from their parents, are saturated, fed up with tales about their family "background"; they are tired of hearing about "family heritage" and are all too anxious to discredit the "respectable" members of the family history. MCA shows conclusively that most children are fed heavy doses during their formative years of socialization about the "achievements" and "righteousness" of their family. Consistent with the charges of "hypocrisy," the children claim that the "bad side" has been neglected: the "dark secrets" are kept dark and secret, the "black sheep" are dropped quickly from discussion — if they are mentioned at all. Yet, THIS IS THE KIND OF INFORMATION THE YOUNG REBELS WANT TODAY.

Young people today would like nothing better than the chance to show their families that they are hypocrites and liars, and that the parents' secrecy and dishonesty are largely responsible for the state of affairs in the world today. At the same time, the young want honestly to know about the "black sheep" for *positive* reasons: they are potential heroes, defiers of establishment rules — and people to be admired, so the logic runs, simply for being rejected by the rest of the family.

Turning Respectability on Its Head

Today if you tell a youngster that his grandfather was a banker, he'll probably call him a "capitalist pig" and want to know whom he "exploited." Likewise, to tell a youngster about his "hardworking uncle" or "aunt who turned nun" will, more likely than not, evoke responses such as "he was a fool to work hard — for what!!??" Or "she probably became a nun because she couldn't get a guy." Today the youngsters want to know about "others" in the family.

MCA Classification of Black Sheep

MCA has compiled vast amounts of information on a random sample of 3200 families, which conclusively demonstrates that "all" families (97%) have easy-to-discover "black sheep," "outsiders," "criminals," and "perverts" studding the family tree. To cite just a few common examples, almost every family has *at least one* of the following in the family history; horse thief, pimp, gambler, drunk, convicted felon, gunrunner, and homosexual. Less frequently occurring, but recurring, are the following: aunts bearing children out of wedlock, grandfathers who ran illegal distilleries at home, usurers, drug-dealers, scabs, venereal disease victims, certified psychotics, political rebels, incorrigible cousins, and prostitutes — both female and male!

The Service in Action: The Young

Here's how the Service would work: the client gives the Service information about the family in question. If the client has no one special he wants to know about, the Service provides him with a "general family genealogy," stressing the importance in the family line of the most disreputable, infamous members.

If the client wants someone specifically researched — say someone who has been defined by family members as "highly respectable" — the Service accommodates the client, adjusting the fee to the ease or difficulty in gathering the appropriate information which would tend to discredit the individual in question.

Following such research would be a written statement delivered to the client, stressing the most negative aspects of the individuals in question. A special feature of this report, for an added fee, would be an "implication section" in which "innuendos" and "accusations" are hinted at when facts are not available to make a solid disreputable claim.

The Older Children

MCA shows that children between the ages of 30 and 50 are extremely *guilty* about their relationship to their parents. These individuals have a need to feel guilty and thus inflict pain on themselves. The 30 to 50 age group, as countless psychiatric case studies have shown, is in a very strong "double-bind" conflict situation which manifests itself as the simultaneous expression of love *and* hate for the family, of a desire to break away *and* be accepted. Much of this "double-bind" conflict is subliminal, and one of the tasks of the I.G.S. would be to bring this conflict to consciousness and then emphasize the Service as a means of satisfying the need to feel guilty. For this age group a different language would be employed than for the very young, a language which is "softer" but which gets the information across.

CHAPTER FIFTEEN

Macabre Service

Service

Macabre Service

Function and Nature

An in-person amusement service offering both personalized horror experiences and a series of horror chambers to allow individuals to satisfy their craving for extreme horror.

Market Creation

Today's amusement-seeking audiences are being attracted to the panorama of bloody and frightening events that attack our senses daily — war, car accidents, airplane disasters, cult murders are just a few — and the cumulative result of these events is that *horror has become a commonplace in our society.* Modern motion pictures routinely depict scenes of decapitation, savage rape, and violence, while the old horror movies of Lon Chaney, Bela Lugosi, and Boris Karloff are inadequate "comedies" for the modern, macabre imagination. The Macabre Service — providing extreme horror within an "amusement" context — goes beyond the "horror commonplace" to excite anew today's mass horror-seeking audiences.

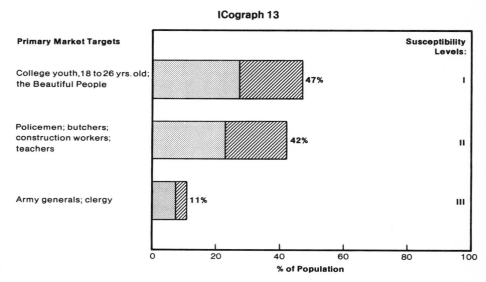

ICograph 13

Primary Market Targets

Susceptibility Levels:

College youth,18 to 26 yrs. old; the Beautiful People — 47% — I

Policemen; butchers; construction workers; teachers — 42% — II

Army generals; clergy — 11% — III

0   20   40   60   80   100

% of Population

Exposition

Background

Recent advances in film technology and human imagination have made the old-style horror thriller of the Karloff days inadequate for a growing audience demanding cannibalistic bloodletting, decapitation, and flaming human flesh. A generation has emerged which has grown *weary* of the usual assemblage of dying and diseased war victims flashing nightly on the television screen at dinner time. This reaction may be termed the *Horror-Commonplace. No longer can vicarious experience satisfy the macabre need. Their experience must be personal.* The Macabre Service is suited to this task.

Staffing and Facilities

Needed are brain-lesion psychologists specializing in violence, horror movie actors, deformed and handicapped personnel (e.g., former circus sideshow performers), a legal staff, and a management staff. The main Service facility will be a *Macabre Center* housing the *horror chambers,* and for all the *personalized horror scenarios* (*see* below) the Service will provide, *facilities* will be arranged for the client (e.g., ghost towns, deserted army barracks, caves, the Empire State Building at night, etc.).

How the Service Works: The Scenario System

A client phones in and makes an appointment. If undecided about his horror desire, he will be sent to consult with a staff psychologist, who will make a recommendation. The client who craves a *specific* experience, as well as the general horror seeker, is guaranteed satisfaction. The client may request one, two, three, or more horror experiences in a three-hour (any time-span) period, and if desired, the client will encounter the *unexpected.* For the less daring, the Service will leave nothing to the imagination and will inform the client in advance of every act that will occur. A client, such as a cavalier executive, may, for example, request to have a disfigured wolf-man stalk and then attack him and his girlfriend while they are spending a weekend in an isolated country area. The Service "wolf-man" will be directed by the Service as to just what kind of attack to perform and when to stop. If, for instance, the client tells the Service that the "wolf-man" should stop *after* his girlfriend faints, the "wolfman" will not stop the attack until the girlfriend really does faint.

Other Horrors: The Macabre Center

At the Macabre Center, the main Service Facility, a "horror chamber" series will be provided. For example, here's how one program, "The Human Flesh Chamber," might appear. As the client sits in the middle of a circular fluorescent chamber, he suddenly becomes bombarded by sounds and horror projections all around him. The "experience" includes the sounds and sights of human flesh burning and people vomiting as their tongues sizzle. The projections could include flesh-eating humans in a horror orgy of cannibalism, gnawing away at already rotting human and animal carcasses and severed heads. The montage might also include female vampires greedily draining green blood from dying and poison-infected animals. Included in the "horror series" could be airplane disaster, war, snakes, drowning, sexual bestiality (for those over 18), and disease chambers.

Horror Vacations: An Added Feature

The Service could easily plot a *sequence horror vacation* for clients who desire to be horrified at intervals while they are traveling.

Spin-off Market

Fashion

MCA predicts that within one year, after expansion of the Service into foreign countries, the horror-service industry will become ubiquitous, so much so as to stimulate the need for a new fashion rage — the *Horror Look*. Such items as flesh-eaten nylons, and an entire series of "body-horror cover-ups" (e.g., lacerated chins) are just around the corner. It is expected that *Women's Wear Daily* will pace-set the Horror Look.

Employment Center for the Deformed

For the entrepreneur with humanitarian inclinations, an employment center can be provided for an estimated 2.7 million deformed individuals seeking dignified employment.

CHAPTER SIXTEEN

Neighborhood Reality-Exploration Service

Service

Neighborhood Reality-Exploration Service

Function and Nature

An in-person educational/visitation/exploration service (e.g., visiting ghettos, participating in riots) to provide new life-style experiences to the culturally deprived middle classes; provide knowledge about alien cultural groups (e.g., Canadian Indians); provide assistance in cultural adaptation and neighborhood integration.

Market Creation

The Neighborhood Reality-Exploration Service is designed to contribute to man's pressing needs for new experiences. This Service is seen as the *inevitable* replacement of outdated educational systems and many vacation services. It is recognized today that individuals feel a pressing need, for a variety of reasons, to experience life-styles not easily accessible to them, such as the millions of liberals in our society who sincerely want to know what life is "really like" in a Black Ghetto, or those who desire to experience the sunrise-to-sunset existence of the migrant grape-pickers. The N.R.E.S. will arrange for "visitations" such as these, ensuring that all events desired by the client actually happen (e.g., being attacked by flea-infested and ravenous rats) in an agreed-upon amount of time. MCA indicates that within a period of years, the Service will eliminate approximately 57% of traditional university services and that, within a shorter time, it will develop internationally.

Exposition

Background

We have learned from the social sciences that *man socially constructs his "real" world* and shapes it to his needs. We have also learned that man is *limited* by his experiences: that is, by the information he receives about the world, and by the manner in which he *interprets* this information.

There is a common expression that *the grass is always greener on the other side of the fence.* This refers to the belief that perhaps one is missing out on something; it refers also to the fact that we are *culture-bound* and that we crave *reality exploration.* The "I-Wonder-What-It-Might-Be-Like" syndrome has perhaps become man's new impetus for understanding his fellow man as the world gradually becomes a "global" village in search of survival mechanisms.

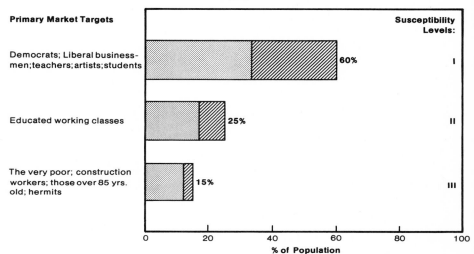

In a sense, man's *unlimited* "imagination potential" (consistent with all ICological principles) is being stimulated by recent ethnic and racial culture-explosions, but certainly needs further stimulation through *real* experiences.

Man has the *natural* desire *to explore*, but unfortunately has believed that many experiences were reserved only for the world of dreams and speculation. The Neighborhood Reality-Exploration service is a first step to bring out *creatively* what has been *natural for ages* but which has been *repressed*: real-life, firsthand experience of "alien" cultures and life-styles.

Service Structure

The Service is to be organized as follows. A Reality Control Center will be the main coordinating unit, where the activities of a *system of neighborhood agencies* will be properly sanctioned. The neighborhood agencies will have five main departments: (1) *research,* (2) *communiteer,* (3) *guide,* (4) *sleuth,* and (5) *trouble-shooting eclectic squad.* The staff of each of these agencies will be comprised of community peoples such as neighborhood sociologists, psychologists, graduate research trainees, detectives (e.g., for the sleuth department), known militants, priests, rabbis, landlords, professors, travel bureau personnel, and the average person in the community (the "communiteer"), who will volunteer his own special *experiential domain.* The "communiteers" will offer, among other things, lecture tours, home visitations, religious services, tenant-landlord scenarios, "rap" sessions, publicity-on-tour services, and riot-participation scenarios to clients such as educators, administrators, leisure activists, intellectuals, students, housewives, and politicians. The service, then, would be a system of *decentralized* units, offering different programs.

Reality-Exploration Guides

In order to aid the explorer to acquaint himself with his community and to "go native," each agency would be responsible for creating "reality-exploration guides," subject to approval by the Reality Control Center. For example, *argot* (language peculiarities) *portfolios* would sensitize the "explorer" to the "in" words and phrases of the community to be explored, such as the current slang of the Hopi Indians. Other portfolios might become a part of the *"guide,"* such as food, clothing, housing, job, revolution, and recreational. In addition to the portfolios, psychological testing kits and *"role paraphernalia"* might be included in the client's guide. For example, if an individual desired to simulate the role of a policeman, a uniform and accessories would be provided. It is important that the entrepreneur realize that since a client might not *really* know what and how he wants to explore, a well-equipped research department is necessary to help him decide.

A Note on Infinite Reality

Because *reality* is *multiple,* forever changing, and therefore *infinite,* the entrepreneur who starts this service must be prepared to expand in conformance with the IC-Principle. For example, since the Service will advertise itself as a *Neighborhood* Reality-Exploration Service, there is no problem except the matter of how to expand the services into *other areas* (such as mental institutions, leper colonies, and even outer space). However, within the framework of the Service, *exploration will be infinite.* This means that the client may delineate *any kind of reality need,* and *the Service will provide it for him!*

Using the Service

Here is how the Service works: A client may phone in knowing what program he desires or he may desire assistance from the Service. After coming to the Service headquarters and filling out information forms, he proceeds to the research department for an *exploration potential analysis and/or consultation* (for those needing suggestions). The purpose of the analysis is to provide the guide department with information to prepare a *personalized reality-exploration guide*. This aspect of the Service is indeed an exceptional improvement over present educational techniques which are standardized and thus *do not* suit the needs of most *individuals*.

The Role of the Sleuths and Troubleshooters

While the client is on his voyage through the community of his/her choice, the Service will dispatch *exploration sleuths*, whose function will be to see that all is going well with the explorer. For example, if the client was sent to a ghetto expecting a *riot*, but instead encountered only docile, drug-spaced young Blacks sitting around on stoops, the exploration sleuths would immediately report this "discrepancy" to the Service Center, who would then send word to the *troubleshooting eclectic squad department*. The role of the troubleshooters is to "fix" the discrepancy; thus, in this example, they would *immediately induce a riot condition!* Only through a process such as this can client satisfaction be guaranteed.

Further Illustrations of Poverty-Exploring

1. A wealthy business executive who has lived in luxury all his life might desire to experience the poverty condition. The N.R.E.S. would provide him with a personalized exploration program to enable him to feel the consequences of being poor. A program might include residence-in-squalor with a ghetto family, eating only once a day, being bullied by neighborhood police and drug-pushers, searching for cigarette

butts, and sleeping in a bed crawling with lice and bedbugs. 2. A Montauk "housewife," for years has been plagued by excruciating boredom. When approached about her views and desires concerning Neighborhood Reality Exploration, she was ecstatic. She had always wanted to participate in a *social-work program* in a ghetto area. What did it feel like being a social worker? She desperately wanted to know.

At the Neighborhood Reality-Exploration Service, she could ask for a social-worker "guide," which might include a psychological testing kit, a narcotics commission check-off list of poisonous and dangerous drugs, a supply of nickels, a furniture portfolio, and a social-work notebook with prepared questionnaires. She could immediately proceed to a "five-family" area where she could encourage, discuss, and perhaps even *save* the families into success. If she desired, for an additional contract clause with the Service, she could obtain the rights for visiting the same five families in two years and to publish her memoirs of social-worker experience.

Franchising

One of the brightest prospects of this enterprise is that there is an exceptional foreign market. For instance, there are approximately 225,000 Indians in Canada, many on reservations, who might welcome a franchise to provide reality exploration of their culture. For example, a client could phone the central board of the Reality Control Center and ask for an area to explore which has (1) Indians, (2) teepees, (3) Indian agents, (4) many bars, etc. He could immediately be transferred to an Indian reservation in Canada and could make arrangements for an exploration. The same process would apply to those wishing to explore Middle East refugee camps, Peruvian jungle colonies, Beverly Hills, etc.

The Vacation Market

MCA shows that the Neighborhood Reality-Exploration Service will present an unprecedented challenge to present vacation markets. As the Service develops (visits to prisons, work camps, homes for the aged, army compounds, etc., anywhere in the world), the intellectual component will be brought to the travel market for perhaps the very first time.

CHAPTER SEVENTEEN

"Hang-Up" Service

Service

"Hang-Up" Service

Function and Nature

An in-person therapeutic service to enable individuals with recognized "hang-ups" to redefine their "hang-ups" as virtues; make "hang-ups" fashionable; discover new "hang-ups."

Market Creation

Modern man, being constantly labeled "pathological," "neurotic," or "deficient," *needs to be vindicated.* Psychiatry has *dismally failed*, and what is needed is an alternative. The "Hang-Up" Service will correct the injustice perpetrated on man's search for individuality by redefining behaviors traditionally defined as "hang-ups" (such as being short, being shy, being frigid, etc.) as virtues. Indeed, even a growing number of psychiatrists are calling attention to the greatly outmoded *priest-sinner relationship* fostered by their form of treatment, and MCA shows that many would be readily available to help staff the new enterprise of *"reverse-therapy"* and the science of *"individualism-approval."* This Service would become an overnight declaration of a revolutionary new independence, becoming the new cornerstone of individual faith.

ICograph 15

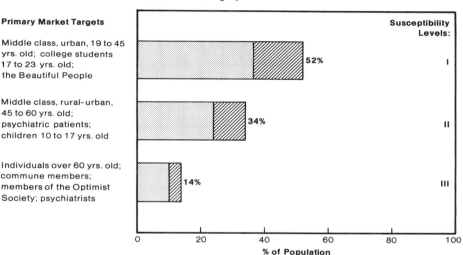

Primary Market Targets

Middle class, urban, 19 to 45 yrs. old; college students 17 to 23 yrs. old; the Beautiful People

Middle class, rural-urban, 45 to 60 yrs. old; psychiatric patients; children 10 to 17 yrs. old

Individuals over 60 yrs. old; commune members; members of the Optimist Society; psychiatrists

Susceptibility Levels:

I

II

III

52%

34%

14%

0   20   40   60   80   100
% of Population

Exposition

Background

Many times throughout its history, America has been forced to look at itself from the wrong end of the telescope of capitalism, the most critical instance being in the 1930's. At that point, a renewed faith was needed to turn the capitalist instrument around, and gradually, with the encouragement of the academic community, the business world mobilized and worked toward the "perfection" of the capitalist society.

Today, there is a *new crisis*, equal to, if not more severe than, that experienced by a generation that fought discouragement and shock. The youth rebellion, the individual-revolution, and the growing feeling among consumers that the alienation they feel *is not that they fail in what they seek, but that they seek what is clearly not theirs*, present the "spirit of capitalism" with its greatest challenge.

Unfortunately, the pragmatic belief held by the business world, *"do the best with what you've got,"* has not been shared by the psychiatric profession. If this were so, then the multitude of behaviors now defined by psychiatrists and others as "hang-ups" would be seen as virtues — allowing the individual citizen to live a happier, fuller, more creative existence.

The "Hang-Up" Service and Human Potential

The "Hang-Up" Service will not only contribute to the development of TOM, making morality more consistent with the spirit of IC, but will enable the increasingly outdated and disoriented PIC-individual (the individual with a "Post-Industrial" consciousness) to renew his faith in the belief that what he does has value; in fact, what he does (his uniqueness) can also become *fashionable*.

Service Staff

Needed are (1) *discussants* who are well versed in taking case histories; (2) *approvalists* recruited from the behavioral sciences; (3) *researchers* and (4) *reverse-therapists* (drawn from the swelling ranks of renegade psychiatrists). In addition to this professional staff, "reinforcers" are needed (men and women simulating a wide variety of roles in the stage of Reverse-Therapy (*see* example below, "Mr. Z").

Using the Service

A consumer phones in and makes an appointment. Upon arrival at the *Discussion Center* he fills out an assortment of information forms in order to identify and isolate his "hang-ups"; he also talks with a discussant who takes his case history. Eventually, the client will experience all the program divisions as he is led through the stages of: (1) First Approval; (2) Research and Analysis; (3) Second Approval; (4) Reverse-Therapy. From the Discussion Center, the information form is immediately sent to the Research Department and a duplicate form to the Approvalist Department, where a corps of "approvalists" quickly scans the information and designs a "first approval" program for the customer. When the customer enters, *it will be the task of this body to praise him for his individuality.* Meanwhile, the Research Department is busy determining exactly how unique the "hang-up" really is and how it could be made into an "ultimate hang-up unit." For instance, if the customer is a "constant masturbator" but only rarely achieves orgasm, his "uniqueness" may fall somewhere around the middle of the "normal hang-up curve index." It will then be necessary to research and analyze carefully the customer's case history and "hang-up," and to determine exactly what components of the "hang-up" may have been overlooked by the client and which need to be emphasized in order to assure that he has a truly "ultimate hang-up unit potential." For example, if the customer happens to be an economist, and as MCA has shown 67.7% of practicing economists have difficulty ever having an orgasm, the customer could be told that his success ratio is greater than two to one. After research has provided the necessary information about the "hang-up" in question, the customer returns to the Approvalist Department, where he is engaged in initial chatter about his behavior, newly defined as a "virtue." If the "approvalists" contend that the customer is adept at redefining his "hang-up" as a virtue, he is then brought to the Reverse-Orientation Therapy Center (ROTC) for the first test which awaits him. (*See* example below.) *The customer's psyche will now encounter a more symbolic and vigorous reinforcement of his "virtue."* If the customer's response to the reinforcement is positive, then reverse-therapy has succeeded.

A Quick Run Through the Service

Miss X

A woman anxiously arrives at the Service deeply bothered by her appearance. She is 4'11" short and weighs 165 pounds. The task of the Service is not to "cure" her of her appearance-"hang-up," but to redefine her physical condition as a virtue. For example, an "approvalist" may provide her with positive reinforcement, e.g., showing her pictures of famous and respected fat and short women such as Totie Fields, Mama Leone, and Molly Goldberg; following this she is taken to the ROTC (Reverse-Orientation Therapy Center), where upon arrival she is warmly greeted with a standing ovation by hundreds of short, fat women who praise her for her beauty. She is then escorted by a handsome (Service) "Prince" into the dining room of a midtown Schrafft's Restaurant for all to see her. The reverse-therapy ends with a (Service) poet-psychiatrist reciting a romantic sonnet in praise of short, fat women.

A Close-up on Mr. Z

Mr. Z, who is a rapidly deteriorating business executive, has what he considers a depraved "hang-up." (Mr. Z is a friend of the authors). In his early youth, he first experienced sexual pleasure while swinging on a cross bar with his legs crossed. As he matured, he periodically remembered this pleasurable moment, and with this image came another, one that has plagued him for many years. He imagined himself being *flogged* at the hands of a pretty woman. Mr. Z, unable to perform sexually unless this thought stimulated him, never actually put his masochistic desires into practice. When he couldn't adequately conjure up the image of flagellation, his coital performance was dismally unsuccessful. Mr. Z, living in a world abhorring such depraved debauchery, was seeking salvation. Unable to find comfort in traditional psychotherapy, Mr. Z presently is on the verge of a *serious* nervous breakdown. With the creation of the "Hang-up" Service, Mr. Z not only *could have* mental satisfaction resulting from a successful flagellation experience *but could learn to take great pride in the "uniqueness" of his "hang-up."* Here is how the Service could help Mr. Z.

At the Discussion Center, Mr. Z would carefully describe his torturous "hang-up." His case history completed, *he would then be approved for his individuality* by the corps of "approvalists." In search of the *"ultimate hang-up unit potential,"* the research department would utilize the following information given by Mr. Z: (1) that he has the flagellation image when he thinks about the many pretty prostitutes who nightly walk his block, and (2) that he often has the flagellation image when he is chastised by the corner grocery woman. Upon receiving this information, the Approvalist Department (AD), now equipped with the necessary ammunition for further discussing with Mr. Z the *added virtues*, provides the reinforcement necessary for Mr. Z to redefine his "hang-up" as a virtue. *Mr. Z is not merely a masochist, but an inventive masochist.*

A Note on Individualism-Approval

Individualism-Approval is the total science used by the "Hang-up" Service. This includes all stages of approval such as DC discussion sessions and reverse-therapy. The renewed health and conception of self by the client is the vital and necessary contribution of the "Hang-up" Service in these times of moral confusion. The Service will *scientifically* use its resources and imagination to "cure" people like Miss X and Mr. Z of their low self-esteem and reverse their *unjustly defined* "hang-ups" as virtues.

CHAPTER EIGHTEEN

Honesty Anonymous Service

Service

Honesty Anonymous Service

Function and Nature

An in-person group-therapy and psychological consultation service to allow individuals to reveal "deep-buried" secrets anonymously and thus relieve pressures which often result in psychological impairment; facilitate the development of the "honest society"; provide a superior alternative to such ineffective methods of therapy as church confessions and private psychiatry.

Market Creation

The Honesty Anonymous Service is a business and moral response to the need for honesty in our society. For such reasons as "loneliness," "bizarre activities," "sworn secrets," etc., individuals suffer the burden of not being able to *share* information honestly and this often leads to "blowups" and "breakdowns." MCA reveals that many of the nonhonest desire a way to "tell their story" *but* not reveal themselves. This is because they are afraid that such information could be used against them; is "not believable"; is inconsistent with their image, and so on. Nonhonesty may generally be classified in any one of five distinct categories: (1) the sexual, (2) the familial, (3) the "visionary" experience, (4) the sworn secret, (5) the criminal. For expediency and effectiveness, subtherapeutic groups could be formed among individuals who share the same "secrecy area." This, however, would ultimately be decided by the H.A.S. staff of social scientists and psychiatrists who have had sensitivity training in the dynamics of honesty-dishonesty. Chronic dishonesty among human beings guarantees the *permanency* of this Service, and allows for wide latitude in exporting.

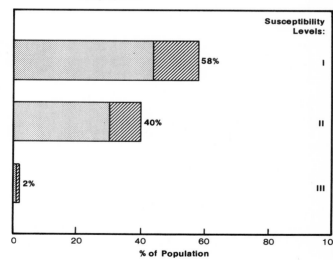

ICograph 16

Primary Market Targets

Susceptibility Levels:

Liberals 16 to 49 yrs. old; the dying; slum landlords; sociologists; life-insurance salesmen — 58% — I

Psychiatric patients; clergymen; compulsive church confessionists — 40% — II

Essalen graduates — 2% — III

0   20   40   60   80   100

% of Population

Exposition

The Need for Honesty

All human beings have a need to *share* ideas — especially ideas which they deem "important." So vital is this need that grave mental and/or physical consequences are likely if the need is not met. Psychiatric casebooks confirm this: many a psychological impairment has resulted *directly* from "keeping things to oneself," from the "pressures of secrecy."

The Nonhonest

There are many reasons why people are not able to share ideas, or share ideas honestly. First, there are the *lonely*: MCA shows there are about 4.8 million people in the U.S. who have *no one to talk to*; second, about 18.6 million people have had something happen to them, or did something, of such an *extraordinary nature* that they "would not tell anyone"; third, there are 1.8 million people who are harboring information they have "*sworn* not to tell": the family secrets, the embarrassing moments, the criminal act, the perverted act, etc.* These reasons and others (e.g., "where does honesty get you?") account for nonhonesty either by *omission* or by *distortion*. And what results from such nonhonesty is oftentimes the "breakdown" or the "blowup."

---

* The 1.8 million figure, of course, does not include government employees, their families and intimate friends.

The Honesty Anonymous Service As a Response to Nonhonesty

What is needed is a service to give people the opportunity to be honest, to share ideas kept buried, to *relieve* themselves. This is the H.A.S. But at the same time this Service must guarantee anonymity if requested by the client; for MCA has noted that many people *must* speak honestly to others — but *cannot* be *identified* (this will become apparent when reading "MCA Categories of Nonhonesty").

Beginning

Certain people will have to be *selected carefully* as "beginners" — to start the Service rolling and to form the "core." These individuals, in addition to wanting personal relief, will have to want to participate in *initiating newcomers* as they begin to arrive. The H.A.S. will be structurally similar to "Neurotics Anonymous," "Smokers Anonymous," etc., in that the *influence of the group* will provide the basis for *cure*. Each nonhonest individual will evoke the honesty in the others.

Staff

The entrepreneur beginning the H.A.S. will cautiously select a staff of psychiatrists, sociologists, and psychologists who, in order to qualify for the position, must first state that their previous work was basically dishonest. If they are unwilling to do so, this means (more than likely) that they are *afraid of truth* — and thus will not be able to "guide" others to honesty. Once the admission is made, however, these people, who have studied the dynamics of honesty-dishonesty, will arrange the sessions among group members, be on hand to treat noncontrollable emotional outbursts, and offer their skills (as part of the Service) to those who wish to begin private sessions of Honesty Therapy.

Maintaining a Secret Identity

Many clients, while revealing the truth, will not want their faces seen for a variety of reasons. Many clients will be revealing truths of such a bizarre nature, of such a scandalous nature, etc., that they will feel *threatened* if "others" *know* who is speaking these things. Thus, they will want to be assured that their personal identity will not be made public. This can be done in any one of several ways.

1. The speaker and audience can be separated by a wall.
2. The speaker can provide a disguise for himself — or the Service can provide the disguise.
3. The Honesty Room can be totally blacked out during the sessions.
4. The group members can be instructed to attend all meetings wearing hoods or masks.

As can be seen, only 3 and 4 allow for *total spontaneity*, as 1 and 2 assume that the speakers are scheduled *in advance* of each meeting. The latter two, however, enable those who must *spontaneously* reveal their secret to do so. Of these we suggest 4, as it allows for greatest all-around *flexibility*.

Making the Public Aware

Many people have so repressed their ideas and information that they have "consciously" forgotten it — but it is a plague on their house. They "know," but they do not *know*. In creating the market for the H.A.S. the "public unconscious" must be reactivated, the demons must be called up. The individual must be *made aware* that his nonhonesty is hurting him, and this must be *strongly associated* with the H.A.S. as the *only* means of psychic and emotional *cure*.

MCA Categories of Nonhonesty

Many people share the *same or similar secrets*, having done the same or similar things, but, by definition, each individual does not know this about the "others."

MCA has been able to classify the dominant categories of *recurring secrecy* shared by large numbers of people. These follow, along with an explanation of their relationship to the H.A.S.:

1. *Sexual secrets* — parents gaining sexual pleasure from their own, infant children, bestiality.

2. *Family secrets* — the embarrassment syndrome: "My father (mother) was a drunk (psychotic, etc.). He made my life miserable . . ." or the "illegitimate" syndrome: "My parents lived together out of wedlock . . ."

3. *Visionary secrets* — "I saw God and He said to me . . . If I ever told anyone they'd think I was crazy. Do you know what I mean?" or "I spoke to my dead husband and he

told me he always hated me and the kids. I had to tell someone."

4. *Sworn secrets* — "I accidentally overheard the talk between Jules and Izzy and they made me promise never . . ." or "My father said he'd kill me if I ever told what I know about how he made his fortune."

5. *Criminal secrets* — murder: "I once killed a man and have had to live with this on my mind." (Note: MCA has shown this to be *much more frequent* than is normally expected.) Or theft: "My brother and I stole from this poor old lady down the block. How could I tell anyone she was our grandmother?"

The H.A.S. will focus on these above categories of individuals in the beginning, forcing them to awareness and then subliminally instilling the need to "reveal" in an atmosphere of anonymity. Once at the Service, the hooded individual will relate the details of the unshared idea carried within for so many years. The words will flow, first slowly, then more quickly, revealing every detail of the buried secret. The group will listen to the individual testimony, offer suggestions, applaud at times, groan at times, encourage "deeper" honesty, and offer congratulations when the secret is out. Honesty will be achieved.

Spin-off Market

The Service can profitably *record the testimony* of the H.A.S. clients, as the information revealed will most often be "sensational." The recorded testimony can then be sold to the *general public* in the form of magazines, records, novels, or tape. In all instances, of course, anonymity will be guaranteed and the clients need not even know about this, as it is of no concern to them. This will result in a spin-off market with minimal sales/yr. estimated at 1,432 million dollars (based on comparison with competing markets and the estimate of sales volume and testimony derived from the H.A.S. itself).

Competing Market

Many people now use psychiatry as a means of honesty-realization, but this is, for the masses, too expensive, too ineffective, divorced from the group context, and *not anonymous!* The H.A.S., once defined as *including* the advantages of psychiatry, *plus* the many added advantages, will find little problem in competing with the psychiatric market and will most likely result in its eventual downfall.

CHAPTER NINETEEN

Aggravation Service

Service

Aggravation Service

Function and Nature

A telephone and/or in-person therapeutic and information service to provide detailed and "instant" analysis of the causes of chronic and/or daily aggravations to enable the client to channel aggressions properly in a rational and satisfying manner.

Market Creation

MCA shows that most individuals are totally ignorant of the sources of their daily and chronic aggravations. To be sure, virtually everyone feels aggravated daily, but few know the *cause* of their irritation. Since the cause is rarely analyzed properly, the *aggressive behavior* which results from aggravation is most often aimed at the *wrong target*. MCA indicates that individuals can be greatly aided in accurately analyzing the sources of their aggravation, thus enabling them to direct hostilities at *appropriate targets*. Once the Aggravation Service is on the market, consumers will become increasingly aware that their hostilities are, and have been, misdirected. Use of the Service will result in increased peace of mind, satisfaction, and efficiency. The Aggravation Service, staffed by *certified* Jungian psychiatrists skilled in dissecting aggravation, will provide the client with a detailed breakdown of the sources of his aggravation. Such information will be represented on an *aggravation chart,* a very special feature of this Service. The chart also allows for at-home self-analysis, and provides for a handsome spin-off market.

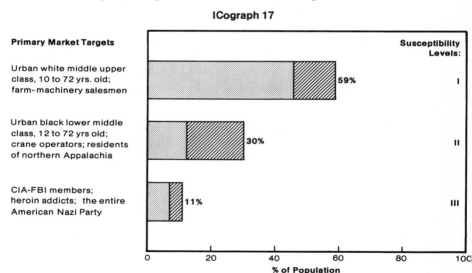

ICograph 17

Primary Market Targets

Urban white middle upper class, 10 to 72 yrs. old; farm-machinery salesmen — 59%

Urban black lower middle class, 12 to 72 yrs old; crane operators; residents of northern Appalachia — 30%

CIA-FBI members; heroin addicts; the entire American Nazi Party — 11%

Susceptibility Levels: I, II, III

% of Population

Exposition

Background

Many people suffering from tension often feel that they are heading for depravity, self-destruction, and insanity. They often seek to reduce these feelings but find that *the more they fight them, the more aggravated they become.* Tension can be seen as an *emotion* deeply rooted in the *complex* world in which we live. Annoyances that might possibly be forgotten or ignored become critical issues and we attack whatever or whoever is convenient. For example, *how many mothers-in-law are victimized yearly?* MCA has shown that many of our temperamental reactions are overexaggerated and our aggravations are oftentimes completely unrelated to the object of our hostile attention. Sometimes, the everyday tensions become compounded because they are not properly channeled. The Aggravation Service is designed to provide detailed and "instant" analyses of the causes of aggravations to enable the client to release his aggressions in a *responsible* and *rational* manner.

Staffing the Service

Needed are dramaturgic sociologists, ecotactic specialists, computer programmers, an A-1361-TX computer, and Jungian psychiatrists.

The Service in Action

After an appointment has been scheduled, the client, dramaturgical sociologist, and Jungian psychiatrist discuss, in depth, the client's "aggravation history." When this is completed, a process dependent upon *immediate* client sincerity and honesty which should take no longer than 2 to 4 days, the "aggravation history" is fed to the A-1361-TX computer for "structural aggravation analysis." The result is a computer print-out personalized *aggravation chart* — a systematic analysis of tension spots — such as relationship with the boss, attitude toward rush-hour traffic, sexual virility — with *percentages* attributed to the various sources of aggravation. In this manner, the probability that hostilities *may be* channeled in a rational manner is greatly increased, and misplaced aggravation, the kind most responsible for compounded tensions, will be at a minimum. The A.S., then, provides *probabilistic* (%) aggravation targets, and unlike outdated psychiatry and psychiatric therapy, analysis is "instant."

Quick Aggravation Analysis

Once the structural analysis has been completed and stored in the memory bank of the computer, the client may *phone in* for analysis of *new* and/or *passing* aggravations which may be plaguing him on any given day. For example, Mr. X may receive a quick analysis which indicates that his mother-in-law was 78% responsible for his migraine headache and his father-in-law 18% responsible. Once he has this information, the decision for *action* rests with Mr. X. The Service is protected against any indictment for assault, murder, etc., as responsibility for action decisions rests with the client.

Spin-off Market: The Aggravation Chart

The *aggravation chart,* allowing for *at-home self-analysis* through a program of carefully selected psychological questions and general guidelines, is a natural spin-off product. While not as in-depth as the analysis provided at the Service, the at-home analysis will provide for considerable enlightenment and cut down the number of hostile acts directed at wrong targets. The user will answer questions aimed at isolating sources of aggravation and will carefully attribute precise target *percentages* — as indicated on the chart — to all "sources" to see if there is an emergent and/or recognizable pattern.

Even though the chart will be an extremely successful product, MCA shows that the Aggravation Service will continue to serve as the center of professional Aggravation Analysis.

CHAPTER TWENTY

Saturation Service

Service

Saturation Service

Function and Nature

An in-person individualized therapeutic and/or amusement service to provide fast, effective cure for those suffering from a particular repetition-compulsion, e.g., constantly picking the "scab" off sores; provide amusement for those who enjoy but can't get enough of their particular repetition-compulsion.

Market Creation

The repetition-compulsion, a neurosis which afflicts virtually *all* human beings, is a source of pain to some, and a potential source of pleasure to others. The Saturation Service, which is designed to cater to the special needs of compulsive-neurotics, provides either "cure" (to those suffering pain) or amusement (to those seeking pleasure). This Service operates on the principle of "saturation" — which essentially means giving the neurotic *all he/she desires of a particular thing* — whatever it is — and then, via different techniques, either "satisfying the neurosis" or "curing the neurosis." The latter is accomplished by the method of "beyond saturation" and offers a quick and effective alternative to psychiatry. This Service has the potential to appeal to all human beings, in all countries, since the need to which it is a response is *universal.* The Service would not only cater to such commonplace repetition-compulsions as turning off the gas jets on stoves, picking one's nose, zipping up the fly on one's pants, and so on.

ICograph 18

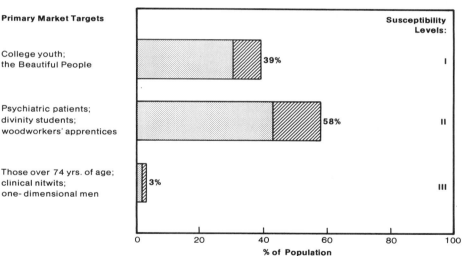

Primary Market Targets

Susceptibility Levels:

College youth; the Beautiful People — 39% — I

Psychiatric patients; divinity students; woodworkers' apprentices — 58% — II

Those over 74 yrs. of age; clinical nitwits; one-dimensional men — 3% — III

0   20   40   60   80   100

% of Population

Exposition

A Universal Neurosis

A great deal of evidence suggests that virtually all human beings are *compulsive neurotics:* this means that *we* all *repeat* certain behaviors *continually* — oftentimes against our better judgment and against our own will (e.g., continually pulling out the alarm-clock plunger when we know damn well it's out!). Thus, the neurosis has been labeled by psychiatrists the "repetition compulsion."

Two Types of Compulsive Neurotics

MCA, after studying this phenomenon, concludes that human beings divide fairly evenly into two groups: (1) there are those who are greatly disturbed by their particular repetition-compulsion and *desire to get rid of it;* (2) there are those who derive *pleasure* (albeit neurotic) from their repetition-compulsion and *want to retain it and have it continually satisfied.*

The Saturation Service is designed to cater to both groups of individuals.

The Saturation Service Defined

The Saturation Service will function differentially depending upon whether the client wishes to *retain* and *satisfy* or *cure* the repetition-compulsion in question. In either case, the basic method of the Service is to provide the client with *whatever it is* that the neurosis is centered on — and "saturate" him with it until he has been "satisfied" (pleasure has been attained) or "cured" (a disgust for the behavior has been achieved). To accomplish this end, the Service will require a versatile staff consisting of sado-masochistic personality types (who will derive pleasure when taking the client "beyond saturation" (*see* "Some Examples," Part 2) who have been trained in the psychological sciences. The staff will also include physicians to aid the client who has "crumbled" under the saturation experience.

In addition to this staff, the Service must have access to a great variety of equipment and material which will be needed to reproduce events necessary for the successful operation of the Service (this point is illustrated below under "Some Examples").

Some Examples

1. For those who wish to *satisfy* and *enjoy* their repetition-compulsion:

(a) The client phones the Saturation Service and states, "I love to look up women's skirts as they exit from automobiles, and I can't get enough of it." To cater to this client, the Service will arrange to have a bevy of females wearing peek-a-boo skirts especially designed for automobile exits (to reveal just the right amount of thigh, top-of-the-stocking, garterbelt, etc.), and an auto ready when the client arrives at the Service. The client will be comfortably seated, or placed in a "hideaway" spot (as he requests) from which he will watch — *for as long as he desires* — the females exit from the auto.

The fee is adjusted according to time, cost of the "event reproduction," and so on (this fee can be reasonably estimated in advance, save for the "time limit," which will depend on the client's disposition while at the Service).

(b) A female client informs the Service, "I can't get enough of that scene in *Gone with the Wind* when Clark says to Vivian, 'Frankly my dear, I don't give a damn,' only I'm tired of the rest of the picture; I've seen it 117 times already, and I wish I could just see that one scene over and over and over." The Saturation Service easily obliges her and collects a handsome fee.

2. For those who wish to be *cured* of their repetition-compulsion (here, as we shall see, the technique is somewhat different):

A client informs the Service, "I can't get this *tune* out of my head; it's with me all the time and is driving me crazy; I love it and I hate it. *I want to get it out of my head for good.*"

To cure this client, the Service will proceed as follows:

First, the client is greeted cordially and seated comfortably. The tune in question is placed on a recorder and played for the client. Assuming that he initially enjoys hearing it, the Service continues to play it until the client claims that he's had enough and that he's "saturated" for the moment, and requests to leave. At this point, to achieve *cure*, the Service resorts to a special strategy: THE CLIENT IS NOT PERMITTED TO LEAVE.

MCA concludes that to achieve cure (in most instances) the client must be taken *"beyond saturation."* Thus, the client, to continue our illustration, is *strapped in his chair* and the tune is continued. In addition, *the volume is increased!*

At this stage the client will be (usually) extremely annoyed with the Service, but the idea is to cure him — and this is what is being done. When the client begins to appear very disgusted, and looks somewhat ill, a judgment is made by the staff whether or not a cure has been effected (at this stage particularly, the necessity for a sadomasochistic staff is apparent).

When it is decided that the client is cured, he is released and sent home. Depending upon the entrepreneur's own predisposition, cure can be *guaranteed* or not (MCA has concluded that this method is highly effective in 87% of cases tested).

The Service As an Alternative to Psychiatry

The method of cure based upon saturation is relatively inexpensive and is MCA-proven to be more effective than lengthy psychiatric treatment for the repetition-compulsion. Thus, this Service is designed for the modern American on the go who doesn't have the time for, or trust in, traditional psychiatry.

Saturation and General Problems

The method of "beyond-saturation" can be fruitfully employed on individuals seeking cure from such activities as gambling, kleptomania, religious ritualism, and so on. Activities such as these, which have ruined many a family, could be quickly and effectively counteracted by use of the method offered by the Saturation Service.

A Note on the Saturation Service and the Law

Because the saturation-cure oftentimes requires that the client be held at the Service against his will, it is advised that the Service request the client to sign a contract specifying that the method of cure is to be determined by the Service and that ultimate responsibility rests with the client (in "TOM," *see* "IM and the Law").

CHAPTER TWENTY-ONE

Lacquered Umbilical Cord

Product

Lacquered Umbilical Cord

Function and Nature

The umbilical cord accompanying each new birth — procured with the cooperation of hospital administrators and obstetricians — is to be lacquered for longevity and durability to serve as a memento-piece, fashion-piece, and/or "all-purpose household accessory," which allays psychological anxieties of parents that relate to death, aging, child-departure, and power; facilitates socialization of children in the desired direction; enhances the interior decoration of the home; adds a necessary touch of the "personal" in this age of increasing alienation.

Market Creation

The umbilical cord, heretofore defined as waste, may be viewed as an "updated version" of the bronzed baby shoes, with many added advantages. The cord, easy to procure, process, package, and deliver, has the advantage of being nondescript and pliable — thus enabling it to be contoured into an infinite number of designs and patterns. MCA will focus upon revitalizing the same universal sentiments that made the bronzed baby shoes such a market success. Distribution of the cord will proceed most easily through a close working arrangement with hospitals, and MCA reveals that many hospital administrators would consider a "partnership" to varying degrees.

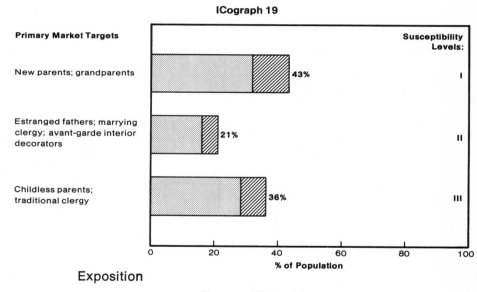

ICograph 19

Primary Market Targets

Susceptibility Levels:

New parents; grandparents — 43% — I

Estranged fathers; marrying clergy; avant-garde interior decorators — 21% — II

Childless parents; traditional clergy — 36% — III

0   20   40   60   80   100
% of Population

Exposition

Bronzed Baby Shoes?

In the year 1902 the first bronzed baby shoes were manufactured. Not long afterwards, such shoes could be found in millions of homes throughout the country. Why? Bronzed baby shoes are nonfunctional, and yet don't serve any public aesthetic function as do paintings, liquor bottles, etc. The shoes are generally "shelved" shortly after purchase. What, then, is the appeal?

The Appeal of Bronzed Baby Shoes

MCA has concluded that there are three primary reasons for the success of bronzed baby shoes:

(1) parents want to *preserve the "special moment."* This is self-explanatory;

(2) parents have a need (as do all aging people) to *stop time in its tracks:* it makes parents *feel younger* and thus *wards off the possibility* (psychologically) *of imminent death* ("Look at those baby shoes, Charley, it seems like only yesterday");

(3) parents have a need to establish, however subtly, a *power hierarchy* between themselves and their child(ren), with the shoes serving as the symbol of the preservation of the status quo (the "bronzing" is solid, sturdy, imperishable — a "frozen" instant).

These *functions* which the bronzed baby shoes serve correspond to the sentiments of the great majority of people (MCA estimate — 72.6% of parents and future parents). But the *shoes* themselves are now defined by most people as *passé:* this is primarily because *objects* are not so important in today's highly *impersonal* world; today it is important to get "inside" people, to have an *organic* relationship with people and loved ones, for *real* meaning. What is needed, then, is something to replace the shoes — some remembrance of the childbirth — but more consistent with the times in which we live; MCA concluded that given the impersonal world in which we live, a highly personal "remembrance" would be just the thing. What was searched for, also, was a product accessible to *every* new parent, thus assuring the immediate success of the newly created business. The umbilical cord is *the* only natural success item.

Advantages of the Cord

First, the cord comes *free of charge* with every child. Second, the cord is easy to transfer from mother to physician to cord-processor. Third, the cord is easy to preserve through a simple process of lacquering. Fourth, the cord is versatile (*see* section below: "Versatility of the Cord"). Fifth, the cord is highly personal — immediately reminiscent of the birth-experience — and simultaneously addresses itself to the same psychological functions fulfilled by the bronzed baby shoes. It can easily be seen how the cord could be advertised to play on people's fears centering on preserving youth, warding off death, preserving the tie between parent and child, and establishing the right of parents to maintain power (status quo) over their offspring (as regards this latter function, the cord could perhaps be endorsed by Billy Graham, Martha Raye, John Wayne and/or other authority figures in our culture).

Versatility of the Cord

Unlike the bronzed baby shoes, which are shoes no matter what is done with them, the cord is a rather nondescript item and is *pliable*. This means that it can be twisted into various shapes (prior to lacquering) or attached to other objects. The cord can either be maintained as a recognizable cord, or used for other purposes, such as a belt (more will be mentioned below).

Because there are so many ways in which the cord can be utilized, a *"Cord Counseling Service"* is suggested here as a possible derivative branch of the cord-processing and manufacturing business. Here are a few illustrations of the Cord's versatility:

1. *The "Religious Cord."* For those who are religiously oriented, and would like to display this in some way, the processed cord could be attached, navel-to-navel, to two *statuettes*, one of a "Mother" and one of a "Child." This is like the "Second Coming" with the client's own cord. Placed on a mantelpiece with a candelabrum behind it, it would be magnificent.

2. *The "Medical Cord."* For parents who want to "hint" that their child should become a doctor, the cord could be easily attached to the metal part of a stethoscope, and the cord draped over the bust of the child. The child would grow up with this image, encouraging his development in the desired direction.

3. *The "Political Cord."* (a) The "Revolutionary Cord" — for parents who want their children to overthrow their government, the child's cord could easily be attached to a statuette of any revolutionary hero (e.g., Lenin, Castro, Marx, Mao, Cleaver, *et al.*). One suggestion would be to have the statuette standing and waving a "dagger" — which is in reality the child's cord. The lacquer could be tinted red for

added effect. (b) Alternatively, for those parents who define themselves as "Good Americans," the cord could be attached to a statuette of Nixon (the "Presidential Cord"), or, if the child is a female, a statuette of Golda Meir, Eleanor Roosevelt, Indira Gandhi, Coretta King, etc., holding the cord (this could possibly be renamed the "First Lady Cord").

The ideas along this line are infinite, and thus counseling could be very helpful. This, perhaps, could be accomplished most easily by first showing the prospective client a catalogue, "The Cord Catalogue," with suggestions (illustrated). Some other uses for the cord, in which the cord is directly utilized as *something* else, are as follows.

1. The "Cord Belt." A chain and hook are simply applied to opposite ends of the cord after processing, and the cord could easily be worn by the child in a few years, or by the parents earlier.

2. The "Cord Necklace." The cord is simply worn around the neck. Hooks could be applied to it, so that the baby's teeth could be attached one by one as they fall out.

3. The "Cocktail-Mixer Cord." Just keep by the liquor counter and use to mix drinks; also good for mixing iced-tea drinks.

4. The "Light-Switch Cord." As the name implies, to be attached to the "switch-on" chain of ceiling lights, closet lights, etc., and pulled each time light is desired. With the first flash of light, the client realizes he is "holding the cord."

Market Permanency

The cord is an item which can be kept permanent with minimal effort so long as it is not initially defined as a "fad."

Biologically and sociologically, there is always a permanent clientele for the cord, and psychologically, there is an increasing need for all that the cord signifies (*see* discussion above on "Psychology and the Cord").

Estranged Fathers and the Cord

Fathers who separate from their wives between the time of conception and the birth of the child are rarely awarded custody of the child. Yet such breakups are frequent (MCA estimate is that this happens in 1 of every 39 childbirths), and oftentimes the father desires the child. Such males could be convinced through very forceful MCA techniques that the cord is a *good second-best*. In this case, the arrangement would be between the cord manufacturer and the father (with the mother's consent, of course) and would necessitate a slightly different, but nonproblematic, approach — especially with regard to distribution and delivery.

A Special Note

MCA has come up with enough evidence via innuendo which suggests strongly that certain hospital administrators and doctors would be *more than receptive* to the idea of "working together" with the cord manufacturer for a *percentage* of the profits — if not a partnership. Needless to say, this was not stated outright, but "suggestions" to that effect were numerous.

CHAPTER TWENTY-TWO

Famous Excrement

Product

Famous Excrement

Function and Nature

A souvenir product provided in pure, natural, and/or blended form and packaged in a jar, frozen or preserved to allow the consumer of celebrity items to identify closely with his favorite public personality (e.g., sports, television, movie, politics, etc.).

Market Creation

A strong consumer need exists for highly personalized products. This is primarily due to the alienated world we live in. In fact, MCA has shown that organic products, although

. . . ad IC . . . ad IC . . . ad IC . . . ad IC . . . ad IC
. . . ad IC . . . ad IC . . . ad IC . . . ad IC . . . ad IC
. . . ad IC . . . ad IC . . . ad IC . . . ad IC . . . ad IC
. . . ad IC . . . ad IC . . . ad IC . . . ad IC . . . ad IC
. . . ad IC . . . ad IC . . . ad IC . . . ad IC . . . ad IC

ad IC . . . ad IC . . . ad IC . . . ad IC . . . ad IC . . . ad IC
ad IC . . . ad IC . . . ad IC . . . ad IC . . . ad IC . . . ad IC
ad IC . . . ad IC . . . ad IC . . . ad IC . . . ad IC . . . ad IC
ad IC . . . ad IC . . . ad IC . . . ad IC . . . ad IC . . . ad IC
ad IC . . . ad IC . . . ad IC . . . ad IC . . . ad IC . . . ad IC
ad IC . . . ad IC . . . ad IC . . . ad IC . . . ad IC . . . ad IC
    . . . ad IC . . . ad IC . . . ad IC . . . ad IC . . .
    . . . ad IC . . . ad IC . . . ad IC . . . ad IC . . .
    . . . ad IC . . . ad IC . . . ad IC . . . ad IC . . .
    . . . ad IC . . . ad IC . . . ad IC . . . ad IC . . .
    . . . ad IC . . . ad IC . . . ad IC . . . ad IC . . .
      . . . ad IC . . . ad IC . . . ad IC . . . ad IC . . .
      . . . ad IC . . . ad IC . . . ad IC . . . ad IC . . .
      . . . ad IC . . . ad IC . . . ad IC . . . ad IC . . .
      . . . ad IC . . . ad IC . . . ad IC . . . ad IC . . .
        . . . ad IC . . . ad IC . . . ad IC . . . ad IC . . .
        . . . ad IC . . . ad IC . . . ad IC . . . ad IC . . .
        . . . ad IC . . . ad IC . . . ad IC . . . ad IC . . .
        . . . ad IC . . . ad IC . . . ad IC . . . ad IC . . .
          . . . ad IC . . . ad IC . . . ad IC . . . ad IC . . .
          . . . ad IC . . . ad IC . . . ad IC . . . ad IC . . .
          . . . ad IC . . . ad IC . . . ad IC . . . ad IC . . .
          . . . ad IC . . . ad IC . . . ad IC . . . ad IC . . .
            . . . ad IC . . . ad IC . . . ad IC . . . ad IC . . .
            . . . ad IC . . . ad IC . . . ad IC . . . ad IC . . .
            . . . ad IC . . . ad IC . . . ad IC . . . ad IC . . .

IC